THE TIME OF THE TOAD

The Time of the Toad

A Study of Inquisition in America

and Two Related Pamphlets

DALTON TRUMBO

PERENNIAL LIBRARY
Harper & Row, Publishers
New York, Evanston,
San Francisco, London

"The Time of the Toad" was first published by The Hollywood Ten in 1949 and is here reprinted by arrangement with the author.

"The Devil in the Book" was first published by the California Emergency Defense Committee in 1956 and is here reprinted by arrangement with the author.

"Honor Bright and All That Jazz" first appeared in the 100th Anniversary issue of the *Nation* and is here reprinted by permission of the *Nation;* © 1965 by the *Nation.*

 For information address Harper & Row, Publishers, Inc., 101 East 53rd Street, New York, N.Y. 10022. Published simultaneously in Canada by Fitzhenry & Whiteside Limited, Toronto.

FIRST EDITION: PERENNIAL LIBRARY 1972

LIBRARY OF CONGRESS CATALOG CARD NUMBER: 72-76980

STANDARD BOOK NUMBER (PAPERBACK): 06-08268-5

A hardcover edition of this book is published by Harper & Row, Publishers

For
Cleo Beth Fincher
whose husband I am

Contents

"the battle for one's legal rights is the poetry of character"

Rudolph von Jhering

THE TIME OF THE TOAD

The Time of the Toad
A Study of Inquisition in America

SOME TIME before he became involved in the Dreyfus Affair, Emile Zola wrote an article called "The Toad." It purported to be his advice to a young writer who could not stomach the aggressive mendacity of a press which in 1890 was determined to plunge the citizens of the French Republic into disaster.

Zola explained to the young man his own method of inuring himself against newspaper columns. Each morning, over a period of time, he bought a toad in the market place, and devoured it alive and whole. The toads cost only three sous each, and after such a steady matutinal diet one could face almost any newspaper with a tranquil stomach, recognize and swallow the toad contained therein, and actually relish that which to healthy men not similarly immunized would be a lethal poison.

All nations in the course of their histories have passed through periods which, to extend Zola's figure of speech, might be called the Time of the Toad: an epoch long or short as the temper of the people may

First published as a pamphlet in 1949.

permit, fatal or merely debilitating as the vitality of the people may determine, in which the nation turns upon itself in a kind of compulsive madness to deny all in its tradition that is clean, to exalt all that is vile, and to destroy any heretical minority which asserts toad-meat not to be the delicacy which governmental edict declares it. Triple heralds of the Time of the Toad are the loyalty oath, the compulsory revelation of faith, and the secret police.

The most striking example in recent history of a nation passing through the Time is offered by Germany. In its beginnings in that unfortunate country the Toad was announced by the shrill voice of a mediocre man ranting against Communists and Jews, just as we in America have heard the voice of such a one as Representative John E. Rankin of Mississippi.

By the spring of 1933, the man Hitler having been in power for two months, substance was given his words by a decree calling for the discharge from civil service of all "who because of their previous political activity do not offer security that they will exert themselves for the national state without reservation," as well as those "who have participated in communist activities . . . even if they no longer belong to the Communist Party or its auxiliary or collateral organizations," and those who have "opposed the national movement by speech, writing or any other hateful conduct" or have "insulted its leaders."

Thereafter, in a welter of oaths, tests, inquisitions, and inquests, the German nation surrendered its mind.

Those were the days in Germany when respectable citizens did not count it a disgrace to rush like enraptured lemmings before the People's Courts and declare under oath that they were not Communists, they were not Jews, they were not trade unionists, they were not in any degree anything which the government disliked—perfectly aware that such acts of confession assisted the inquisitors in separating sheep from goats and rendered all who would not or could not pass the test liable to the blacklist, the political prison, the crematorium.

Volumes have since been written telling of the panicked stampede of German intellectuals for Nazi absolution: of doctors and scientists, philosophers and educators, musicians and writers, artists of the theatre and cinema, who abased themselves in an orgy of confession, purged their organizations of all the proscribed, gradually accepted the mythos of the dominant minority, and thereafter clung without shame to positions without dignity. Of such stamp are the creatures in all countries who attempt to survive the Time of the Toad rather than to fight it.

If the first street speeches of Adolf Hitler may be said to have begun the Time in Germany, then June 7, 1938, signaled the approach of the Toad into American life; for on that day the House of Representatives under a resolution offered by Mr. Martin Dies of Texas, established by a vote of 181 to 41 the House Committee on Un-American Activities.

To outline in exampled detail the conduct by which

the committee thus far has soiled over a decade of American history would merely be to repeat the obvious and to belabor the known. As a matter of general policy it has flouted every principle of Constitutional immunity, denied due process and right of cross-examination, imposed illegal sanctions, accepted hearsay and perjury as evidence, served as a rostrum for American fascism, impeded the war effort, acted as agent for employer groups against labor, set itself up as censor over science, education, and the cinema and as arbiter over political thought, and instituted a reign of terror over all who rely in any degree upon public favor for the full employment of their talents.

Throughout the whole period of its existence the committee has been under attack, not only by progressive and liberal-minded persons, but by all persons of whatever political party who despise unbridled authority and believe in the reality of Constitutional procedure. The most distinguished enemy of the committee was Franklin D. Roosevelt, who rarely overlooked an opportunity to denounce its methods and objectives. Practically every other respected public figure has similarly made known his hostility to the committee.

In addition to individuals, a very large number of bar and ministerial associations, civic groups, trade unions, guilds, and professional and academic bodies have besieged the Congress with resolutions criticizing the committee or demanding its abolition. The principal law reviews of the country have published extensive articles calling attention to the destruction of civil rights wrought by the committee and its agents. The issue repeatedly has been carried to the electorate, and time and again committee members have been retired from public life, indicating the temper of at least some of the people on a fundamental issue.

But neither denunciation nor resolution nor defeat at the polls has diminished the committee's hold upon American life. During eleven years of incessant criticism its budget has increased from $25,000 to $200,000 per year, while its status has changed from temporary to permanent. It stands today as the employer of at least seven investigators in addition to its clerical workers. Possessed of dossiers on millions of Americans, it is more powerful, more feared and more determined than ever it was before.

What, then, is the secret of such power? It lies in the right, which the committee has arrogated to itself at the expense of the Constitution, to inquire into the realm of political thought, affiliation and association. It lies specifically in the asserted right of the committee to ask a single question—"Are you now or have you ever been a member of the Communist party?" —a question to which thirty years of propaganda has lent a connotation so terrible that even the asking of it, regardless of the answer given, can imperil a man's career and seriously qualify his future existence as a citizen free from violence under the law.

How then, since group resolutions and public denunciations and electoral defeats have not affected the committee's usurpation, can its immense power be destroyed? It can be destroyed only if it is flatly challenged; only if the dread question is faced and the servile answer refused; only if the courts, by reason of the individual's refusal to surrender to the committee, are obliged once and for all to rule on the validity of the Bill of Rights as opposed to that of any inquisitorial body however constituted.

Men may yearn for easier ways to halt the encroachments of government upon the individual, but in the final moment there are none. Placed on the stand before this committee, a man must either collaborate with its members in their destruction of civil rights, or by his refusal attempt to destroy the committee's fraudulent power and mark out its limitations. After all the resolutions and denunciations and political campaigns have failed of their purpose, there is no other choice. At this ultimate point of conflict either the committee or the individual is bound to be destroyed.

Mr. Bernard De Voto, writing in the September 1949 issue of *Harper's Magazine*, makes trenchant comments on the committee's recent request to some seventy American colleges and universities to submit to its investigators a list of "textbooks and supplementary reading, together with authors . . . in the fields of sociology, geography, economics, government, philosophy, history, political science, and American literature." Writes Mr. De Voto:

They (the universities) have got to stop the government short right now, that is, if they are not to become bondservants of Congress or in fact of any single Congressman who can swing a majority in the Committee on Rules, Appropriations, Ways and Means, or Un-American Activities. If they abandon as much as one book to Mr. Wood they may as well throw in their hand. They will defy any government control of inquiry whatsoever, or they will be forced to submit to any political dictation, any limitation of academic freedom, and any coercion of academic procedure as a committee majority may care or may be induced to impose. There is no such thing as a partial virgin. There is no such thing as academic freedom that is just a mite restricted. The colleges are entirely free or they are not free at all.

Mr. De Voto's conclusion that one must "defy" the committee or yield to it entirely is correct and inescapable. Such defiance is as important in the sciences and the arts—including motion pictures—as it is in education, since all are concerned with the dissemination of ideas; since all partake, in one degree or another, of the nature of "inquiry."

It was a consideration of just such matters as Mr. De Voto has dealt with which determined the stand of those motion picture writers, directors and producers who were subpoenaed by the Committee on Un-American Activities in October of 1947, to appear as "unfriendly witnesses" in an investigation "to determine the extent of Communist infiltration in the Hollywood motion picture industry."

After the hearings were completed, the unfriendly witnesses, finding it impossible to state their case as news, were obliged to resort to a series of paid advertisements, one of which appeared on November 13, 1947. In this rather expensive variation of a free press, they explained their conduct before the committee in the following words:

> Acceptance of the perverted standards of the committee can result only in creative paralysis, timid ideas and poorer films. Surrender to the committee in any single detail is merely a prelude to total surrender.

It was their action upon this attitude which precipitated the Hollywood blacklist, the contempt of Congress indictments, and the subsequent trials and appeals. The unfriendly witnesses didn't believe there was such a thing as "a partial virgin." They didn't accept the possibility of a free screen that "is just a mite restricted."

* * *

Ranking Republican member of the House Committee on Un-American Activities, and in 1947 its chairman is Mr. J. Parnell Thomas, a New Jersey politician presently under indictment by a Federal Grand Jury for stealing government funds.[1] Mr. Thomas, as a committee fledgling in 1938, became a qualified expert on literary matters by asking a witness "which WPA payroll is Christopher Marlowe on, New York or Chicago?"

1. He was convicted of taking kick-backs from federal employees, a felony, and sentenced to two years imprisonment. Two of his prison mates at the Federal Correctional Institution in Danbury, Connecticut, were Lester Cole and Ring Lardner, Jr., who were serving one year each for a misdemeanor called Contempt of Congress.

The committee's ranking Democrat then and now is Mr. John E. Rankin, who represents the interests of a minority of some five percent of the disenfranchised inhabitants of Mississippi. He is a man who has used the words "kike," "Jew-boy," and "nigger" in open debate on the floor of the House of Representatives.

Members of the committee who appeared from time to time at the Hollywood hearings were Mr. John McDowell of Pennsylvania, since defeated for reelection; Mr. Richard B. Vail of Illinois, since defeated for reelection; Mr. John S. Wood of Georgia, who is the present chairman of the committee and author of its demands for college and university text-book lists; and Mr. Richard M. Nixon of California.

The hearings were held in the Old House Office Building before some eighty representatives of the American and foreign press. They were recorded and broadcast by every major radio network and by innumerable independent stations. They were reported in every capital of the world. A battery of eleven newsreel cameras covered the event for motion picture audiences.

Witnesses were divided into two groups, labeled by Mr. Thomas "friendly" to the committee and "unfriendly." The friendly witnesses were again divided into writers and actors who came principally to accuse; and producers and labor executives who appeared to defend their special interests in the matter at issue.

It would be difficult to imagine more eloquent assertions of loyalty than those made before the committee by the subpoenaed producers:

I feel very proud to be an American. I spent three-odd months in Europe, and I saw the consequence of people who killed laws, who destroyed freedom of enterprise, individual enterprise, private enterprise. . . . I . . . naturally am in favor of anything that is good for all Americans . . . I am for everything you have said . . . it was the statement of a real American, and I am proud of it. . . . I don't think we should be too tense on this. Being too tense, I think you end up without any tense. . . . I find these people have not attacked the government with violence and overthrowing. . . . We will certainly continue, as long as we are in the motion picture industry, to aid this great country of the United States with every ounce of energy we possess . . . I had nothing to do with Russia in 1944. I want no part of it. . . . We rely on a deep-rooted, pervading respect for our country's principles. . . . I can't, for the life of me, figure where men could get together and try in any form, shape, or manner to deprive a man of a livelihood because of his political beliefs.[2]

Or:

I have abundant reason to cherish the blessings of our democracy. . . . If they should find anything detrimental to the American Government or the Congress I would never allow anything against anybody in our government or in our Congress, I would never allow them to have a laugh at such a serious price . . . I have got to confess that was the only time in my life that I gave money to Russia, and if I were to be told that two years ago, God help the one that asked for it. But when they made the

2. Jack L. Warner.

plea that we must go out and help Russia, I felt I would rather they kill Russians than kill Americans and I gave them money. I made the picture in the same spirit . . . I am convinced of that. I am under oath, and if I met my God I would still repeat the same thing.[3]

One there was among the producers—a man of higher intellect and morality than those with whom he had been cast—who declared to the committee:

I can tell you personally what I feel. Up until the time it is proved that a Communist is a man dedicated to the overthrow of the Government by force or violence, or by any illegal methods, I cannot make any determination of his employment on any other basis except whether he is qualified best to do the job I want him to do.[4]

Yet it was this man, upon his return to Hollywood, who accepted the chairmanship of the producer committee to enforce the blacklist. Asked by a *New Yorker* reporter why he had changed his mind, he replied with stark simplicity that he had done it to hold his job. Such is the flavor of toad-meat on the tongue of an aspiring man.

The writers who appeared as friendly, or complaining, witnesses, were of a different stripe. Throughout their testimony ran the plaintive wonder of men who somehow have been passed by in the race for whatever rewards Hollywood may offer:

It is very easy for him [the story editor] to load the [employment] list with Communists . . . [the reader] pre-

3. Louis B. Mayer.
4. Dore Schary.

pares a very bad synopsis of all material submitted by people who are not Communists.[5]

I know anti-Communist writers in Hollywood who have been forced practically to starvation by the refusal of the Communist writers to work for them.[6]

Those members of the Story Analysts Guild (readers) who are sympathetic to or followers of the Communist Party, are in a position to promote, all things being equal, one submitted piece of material coming from people sympathetic to their cause, and to suppress material coming from anybody unsympathetic to their cause.[7]

I wrote a story. They were scared off, and never did the picture . . . Hollywood writers . . . have been scared . . . intimidated.[8]

I was very much in need of money. I have a wife and two children. A job was very precious to me. I sold a producer at Paramount an idea for a story that I had and he hired me and to my joy assigned me to work with ——. . . . But I soon discovered that his (——'s) love of mankind did not extend to me.[9]

I think they should be silenced, deported, or treated as the spies and agents they are. I am the utmost believer in tolerance there ever was, but . . .[10]

Here the motive is clear. These witnesses had enjoyed indifferent success in the sale of their literary creations to the screen, and their employment records were spotty. They wanted the jobs held by the men

5. John Charles Moffitt.
6. Rupert Hughes.
7. James Kevin McGuinness.
8. Rupert Hughes.
9. John Charles Moffitt.
10. Rupert Hughes.

they accused of being Communists, and they forthrightly solicited the aid of the committee in eliminating competition. Despicable, perhaps, or not, as one may view such matters; but certainly not devious, nor beyond the comprehension of reasonable men.

The actors, successful artists all and therefore without private axes to grind, appeared to speak from the deepest wellsprings of patriotism. True, their testimony was prepared by others and carefully rehearsed in advance with Mr. Robert Stripling, committee investigator. But they were eager participants in the show, and their performances seemed to reflect a solemn conviction that their accused fellow-workers were so actively engaged in revolutionary foment that their violent overthrow of the government constituted an imminent peril. Possessed of such convictions—if, indeed, they were convictions—no man may be condemned for voicing them, although the choice of tribunal in this instance may not have been well considered.

By far the most complex of all the friendly witnesses were the two labor executives who, professing widely differing points of view, nonetheless revealed striking similarities as their testimony unfolded. In contrast to the feelings of most men who are invited to participate in such a display, both of them professed their eagerness to testify. "I welcome the opportunity," said the international representative of the I.A.T.S.E.[11] "I would be here, whether you gave

11. Roy M. Brewer.

me a subpoena or not," said the president of the Screen Writers Guild.[12]

Both men, leaders of labor and presumably aware of those acts of Congress which for thirteen years have barred compulsory revelation of trade union membership, appeared zealous to discard such immunities, not only for themselves but for other trade unionists as well. "I see no reason at all why today a man should deny his membership in an American trade union—none at all," said the trade union leader. "I wanted to volunteer the information that I am both a member and serving my third term as president," said the Guild executive, adding that he was "delighted and proud" to do so. Neither man appeared willing to pay even lip service to a tradition of secrecy, the destruction of which, to Negro trade unionists and organizers in the South, often brings swift and violent death.

Still another similarity between the two stood forth in the revelation that each was appearing before the committee for the avowed purpose of winning a union fight in which he was engaged. The I.A.T.S.E. unions at the moment were violating the picket-lines and taking over the struck jobs of painters, carpenters, and story analysts, all of whom the trade union witness accused of being Communists and hence fair game. "We hope," he said, "that with the help of the committee, the Communist menace in the motion picture industry may be successfully destroyed, to the end

12. Emmet G. Lavery.

that Hollywood labor may be spared in the future the strife and turmoil of the immediate past."

The president of the Screen Writers Guild also had a union problem. Elections were shortly scheduled in his guild, and some of the candidates for directorships were those same unfriendly witnesses the committee was indicting for contempt of Congress. The guild executive had himself three times been elected president of the guild with the support of the unfriendly writers. He had also run for Congress in 1946, and had solicited their names as sponsors of his candidacy, used their homes for election speeches, and readily accepted their financial contributions to his campaign chest. But he was presently involved in a coalition with the complaining writers who had already testified, in an effort to defeat his former sponsors in their guild candidacies.

Lest his appearance be misinterpreted as a moral stand against the committee's investigation, Lavery made his position perfectly clear:

> My only concern with respect to this whole proceeding, Mr. Chairman, is merely that people might go back home and think that they have been political martyrs. An election in November which is coming up in our Screen Writers Guild might be seriously affected, and not for the better, if people thought that perhaps government had interfered any more than was necessary in the normal operations of the guild.

How much government interference he felt "was necessary" in the guild he elsewhere revealed by stating that he had "appeared before the FBI voluntarily and had offered to put myself and any records of our guild completely at his disposal at any time." This generous act, performed without consent either of board or membership, established his respect for the privacy of union business: he believed in the principle of the "partial virgin" and had succeeded in making one out of his own bargaining organization.

To Mr. Archibald MacLeish's query, addressed to the nation during the committee hearings—"The question before the country is—can a Committee of Congress do indirectly by inquisition into a man's beliefs, what the Constitution forbids Congress to do directly: And if it can, what is left of the Constitution and the freedom it protects?"—the guild president paid no heed. He was not concerned with the issue raised by Mr. MacLeish: he was impetuous in his desire to answer questions the committee had not even propounded to him: he was willing to forego any obligation to the Constitution and the freedom it protects:

> I have a piece of information that I would like to put in the record on my own motion, and on my own volunteering, because I am not súre as a student of constitutional law whether the committee does have the authority to demand it of me, but let me break the suspense immediately and tell you that I am not a Communist.

He then proceeded to tell the committee what he was.

As the two labor representatives were dismissed, Mr. McDowell thanked them for their cooperation.

"You have been a good witness," he informed the union leader. And to the guild executive he said: "It is a great relief to have you testify, to hear you testify . . . without waving your arms and screaming and insisting that something was being done to you—about the Bill of Rights. It is good to hear somebody from the Screen Writers Guild talk as freely as you have."

Clearly the urgency to defy the committee or to condemn its activities was not strongly upon these men. In the full flux of the Toad, voluntarily and without any compulsion, they surrendered two vital constitutional outposts. Their capitulation served not only to repudiate those witnesses who had refused to bow before the committee; it actually provided the committee with righteous ammunition for the waging of its future campaigns against trade unions, atomic science and—as Mr. De Voto has pointed out with such justifiable concern—academic freedom itself.

Only one other position—aside from that of the unfriendly witnesses—remains to be dealt with: that of Mr. Eric Johnston, president of the Motion Picture Association of America. A series of chronological quotations will serve much better than analysis to illuminate the quality of his mind.

In the opening week of the hearings, in the presence of attorneys for the producers and the unfriendly witnesses, Mr. Johnston said:

As long as I live I will never be a party to anything as un-American as a blacklist, and any statement purporting to quote me as agreeing to a blacklist is a libel upon me as a good American. . . . We're not going to go totalitarian to please this committee.

On the morning of October 27, in a full page news paper advertisement, Mr. Johnston wrote:

One of the most precious heritages of our civilization is the concept that a man is innocent until he is proven guilty.

On the afternoon of October 27, appearing as a witness before the committee, Mr. Johnston said:

Most of us in America are just little people, and loose charges can hurt little people. They can take away everything a man has—his livelihood, his reputation, and his personal dignity. When just one man is falsely damned as a Communist in an hour like this when the Red issue is at white heat, no one of us is safe.

On November 20, before a New York audience, Mr. Johnston said:

Freedom of speech is not a selective phrase. We can't shut free speech into compartments. It's either free speech for all American institutions and individuals or it's freedom for none—and nobody.

On November 26—six days later—in the Waldorf-Astoria Hotel in New York City, Mr. Johnston issued a statement which read:

We will forthwith discharge or suspend without compensation those in our employ, and we will not re-employ any of the ten until such time as he is acquitted, or has purged himself of contempt, and declares under oath that he is not a Communist. . . . In pursuing this policy, we are not going to be swayed by any hysteria or intimidation from any source. We are frank to recognize that such a policy involves dangers and risks. There is the danger of hurting innocent people, there is the risk of creating an atmosphere of fear. Creative work at its best cannot be carried on in an atmosphere of fear. We will guard against this danger, this risk, this fear. To this end we will invite the Hollywood talent guilds to work with us to eliminate any subversives. . . . Nothing subversive or un-American has appeared on the screen. . . .

On December 4, Mr. Johnston appeared before the Golden Slipper Square Dance Club in Philadelphia, to accept its 1947 Humanitarian Award for the film *Crossfire,* produced and directed by Mr. Adrian Scott and Mr. Edward Dmytryk, two of the men just banished, by his own edict, from the Hollywood scene. Mr. Johnston rose to this awkward occasion with these words:

Intolerance is a species of boycott, and in any business or job, boycott is a cancer in the economic body of the nation. . . . Hollywood has held open the door of opportunity to every man or woman who could meet its technical and artistic standards. . . . What (our industry) is interested in is his skill and talent, his ability to produce pictures for the joy and progress of humankind.

A year later, in December 1948, testifying for the defense in the trial of Mr. Lester Cole's suit against the blacklisting by Metro-Goldwyn-Mayer, Mr. Johnston said of the producers' conference which preceded the blacklist:

I then arose and said that, in my opinion, these men would have to make up their minds. I think I used the expression they would have to fish or cut bait—that I was sick and tired of presiding over a meeting where there was so much vacillation.

Comment would becloud the record. Mr. Johnston is as simple and uncomplicated as a million dollars: if he hasn't received them by now it provides a shocking commentary on the gratitude of princes.

* * *

At the outset of the Hollywood investigation, the unfriendly witnesses in a full page advertisement—they spent some $70,000 of their own funds during the hearings in an effort to present their side of the case—left no doubt as to the position they would take when called upon before the committee.

"We propose," read their statement,

to use every legal means within our power to abolish this evil thing which calls itself the House Committee on Un-American Activities and to put an end, once and for all, to the uncontrolled tyranny for which it stands.

Later, after some of their number had appeared before the committee and received citations for contempt, they further elaborated their stand in an advertisement which stated:

The Bill of Rights is so popular an organ in the body politic that no public person dares refrain from paying it perfunctory tribute. It is never questioned until someone demands that it be used. At this point, the opposing forces, having almost forgotten its existence, stand forth again to re-enact the struggle which gave it birth—to determine once more whether it shall be the heart or the vermiform appendix of our Constitutional system.

Almost two years later—the indicted witnesses by then engaged in appeal to the Supreme Court—Mr. Archibald MacLeish writing in the *Atlantic Monthly* for August 1949, struck the same note:

> Revolution, which was once a word spoken with pride by every American who had the right to claim it, has become a word spoken with timidity and doubt and even loathing. And freedom which, in the old days, was something you used has now become something you save—something you put away and protect like your other possessions—like a deed or a bond in a bank. The true test of freedom is in its use. It has no other test.

It ought only to be added that the use of freedom, the actual invocation of the Bill of Rights, is an exceedingly dangerous procedure; and that the paths of men who act, even upon sentiments which receive universal acclaim, lead more often to jail than into the sunlight of public approval.

Judicial opinions protecting the individual from inquisition are many and nobly stated: they go back into the remote pages of English history—"And so long as a man doth not offend neither in act nor in word any law established, there is no reason that he should be examined upon his thoughts or cogitation; for it hath been said in the proverb, thought is free . . ." (Edward's Case: 1421)—and have been brought into present times by living judges. A summary of articles in the most important law reviews since the Hollywood hearings indicates that a considerable majority of contemporary legal opinion supports the theory that no body, however constituted, may ask the questions propounded during the Hollywood hearings by members of the House Committee on Un-American Activities.

If, then, the questions are illegal, and in fact represent an assault upon the Bill of Rights; and if the committee wilfully flies in the face of the Constitution and persists in asking them—who is left to provoke the legal conflict which alone can restore the rule of law? Obviously the witness. At this point he stands in solitude between the Constitution and those who would destroy it. He can surrender or fight. He can assert his rights, or answer the questions.

The question of compulsory revelation of trade union affiliation is not complex. The whole history of organized labor demands that no precedent be set which may, under the compulsion of authority, weaken the right of secret membership. There have been many times in the past when compulsory disclosure led to death; there are in the South even now instances of men lynched for trade union activities; and we have no assurance there may not in the future be other times when violence once more will attend the path of the organized worker.

In addition to Congressional acts which prohibit compulsory disclosure, and the National Labor Relations Act provisions for secret ballot in the choice of unions, there exists in the instance of the Screen Writers Guild a specific statement on the matter.

Mr. Charles Brackett, then president of the guild, testifying in an NLRB hearing on writer representation in July 1938, maintained that the membership list of his organization must be held inviolable and secret because of the possibility, then and in the future, of discharge of members of the guild from their employment.

The question of political affiliation, hedged about as it is with fear and almost tribal dread, is immensely more difficult. If a man is a Communist and denies his affiliation before the committee, he has committed perjury and he will go to jail. If he answers affirmatively, the second question put to him will be "Who else?" If he refuses this answer he is in contempt in the same degree as if he had refused the first, and he will go to jail. If he answers the second, he will be confronted with the third: "Who are your relatives? Your friends? Your business associates? Your acquaintances?" At which point, if he complies, he is involved in such a nauseous quagmire of betrayal that no man, however sympathetic to his predicament, can view him without loathing.

His original affirmative answer will involve him in still other difficulties, unless he has voluntarily and carefully selected the time and place and circumstances of his revelation. He will lose his job. His private life will be invaded by the FBI. His public life will be subject to the chivalry of the American

Legion. His friends and relatives, his associates and merest acquaintances, will be shadowed and harassed —even the most innocent, even those with whom he is in political disagreement.

His compulsory confession will not affect his own destiny alone: it will touch twenty, fifty, a hundred lives, baring each of them to the ugly, discriminatory climate of the age. What had been conceived as a brave and noble act becomes cowardly and ignoble. Beyond this, it is wanton; for it was in anticipation of just such emergencies of the individual at odds with this state that the Bill of Rights was adopted. It was not conceived for the powerful and the popular who have no need for it. It was put forth to protect even the most hated member of the most detested minority from the sanctions of law on the one hand, and of public disapproval on the other. It was written, as Mr. MacLeish has said, to be used.

If, however, a man is not a Communist, he must determine for himself whether, by casting aside the immunity with which he is clothed, he wishes to assist the committee in its pursuit of an illegal end. He must consider the precedent which his act establishes. He must decide whether he wishes absolution and approbation at such hands. He must consider the frightened men of Germany, swarming and sweating to appease the inquisition, and the six million people whom their appeasement delivered over to the executioner. He must consider the texture of the Toad, and its desirability for his children. Then he must say no to the question, or he must not answer at all.

In four tumultuous days—October 27 to October 30—the committee cited ten men for contempt of Congress, charging them with refusal to divulge their trade union and political affiliations. The indicted men had been refused the right of cross-examination; they had been denied the opportunity accorded to others to make statements; they had been refused the right to introduce into evidence those scripts which the committee charged carried subversive propaganda; they had been refused the right to examine the evidence against them. It has been said in the press—indeed, it was said by Mr. Thomas himself—that they made speeches to the committee; but this appears improbable in view of the fact that the official record of the proceedings runs to 549 pages, of which 37 contain the testimony of the ten unfriendly witnesses.

As each man was dismissed from the chair a dossier of his activities was read into the record, there to stand for all time, beyond challenge, beyond legal attack, beyond correction. The dossiers represented the accumulated talent of seven investigators, headed by a former FBI agent, Mr. Louis J. Russell.[13] Citizens who trust their security to the FBI may be interested to discover the quality of Mr. Russell's police work.

13. Later discharged by the committee after reports of improper financial relations with a committee witness.

A sample dossier shows the entire evidence to consist of fifty-five newspaper clippings, eight letterheads, three pamphlets, two open letters, two circulars, one printed program, one advertisement, one novel, one standard reference book—and six unsupported statements, none of them alleging Communist party membership.

The value of such material may fairly be judged by the following accusation in my own dossier:

According to *Variety* of March 14, 1941, page 2, Dalton Trumbo was the author of *The Remarkable Andrew,* which was so anti-British and anti-war that Paramount refused to continue with the picture after paying $27,000 for it.

The facts are different. *The Remarkable Andrew* was a novel written by me for which Paramount paid $30,000. I wrote the screenplay. The picture was produced, and released both here and in England. Mr. Winston Churchill—here I resort to Mr. Russell's concept of evidence, and cite Robert E. Sherwood's *Roosevelt and Hopkins*—thought well enough of the film to cable Mr. Roosevelt in Washington urging him to see it. The novel was published in England, where all the author's royalties were paid over directly by the publisher to the Lord Mayor of London's Fund for the Relief of Bombed-Out British Children.

Climax of each dossier was the reading into the record by Mr. Louis Russell, from what he claimed to be original documents, of the accused man's "Communist Party registration card." Demand was made

—and refused—that the accused be permitted to examine the cards. The most cursory investigation would have revealed that a registration card is not a membership card, nor a duplicate of one, but merely the alleged office record of an alleged card.

The Government, in its trial of the twelve Communist leaders in New York City, has developed the fact that the Communist Party of America was dissolved on May 22, 1944, and became the Communist Political Association. It continued to be the Communist Political Association until July 29, 1945, when it was reconstituted as the Communist Party. Yet the alleged cards introduced into evidence were all "Communist Party" registration cards dated in November or December of 1944 to cover the year 1945. They were "Party Cards" when no party was in existence. "Whether that change of name represented a technicality or an actuality is beside the point," Mr. Ring Lardner, Jr. wrote in the *New York Herald-Tribune.* "Obviously the Communists themselves must have taken it seriously enough to alter their official documents."

No action, performed in the glare of such publicity and under threat of universal reprisal, can be pleasing to everyone. There have been criticisms of the conduct of the ten before the committee, and of their later strategy in the struggle that ensued. Some were justified and some were not. Second performances are always better than opening nights, although it must be remembered in this instance that the cast did not aspire to the roles they essayed. They were dragooned into the play against their wills, and in the absence of more expert performers they were obliged to interpret the piece as they understood it.

The most importunate suggestion made by their most friendly supporters urged them, after having received their citations from the committee, to make announcement of their political affiliations to the press. Such action, dramatic as it might have been, would have negated all that went before. The right to secret political opinion or affiliation is founded upon the right of disclosure by choice, not by coercion. The committee was seeking to destroy people and to censor an entire medium by forcible disclosure of opinion. For the witnesses to have revealed to the press that which they had withheld from the committee would have aided the committee in its objective quite as effectively as direct revelation upon the stand. The accused men made their stand before the committee to reestablish their right of privacy, not only in law but in fact. They actually believed in it.

To assert the right of privacy against committee pressure and immediately surrender it to public pressure would be to render meaningless a principle which must exist not only in law but in life itself; for it is only in the day-to-day actions of living men that laws achieve reality. Privacy in relation to political opinion means secrecy. What principle, then, is served by defending the right of secrecy in law only to reveal the secret in life? In such an event law becomes a meaningless ritual, unrelated to life and unworthy of respect; and those who have invoked it only to cast it contemptuously aside become the betrayers both of law and life.

In April of 1948, two of the indicted ten were brought to trial in the Federal Court of Washington, D.C. A later agreement stipulated that the remaining eight would accept the judgment of the first two as their own. Both defendants were convicted by juries consisting in part of government employees who were required to judge impartially between their employer and the accused in a district which has not recorded an acquittal on any charge involving political irregularity in many years. They were given the maximum sentence of a year in jail and a fine of one thousand dollars. They were not permitted to introduce their allegedly subversive motion picture scripts into evidence; nor were they permitted to prove, through expert witnesses, that control of the ideological content of motion pictures lay not in their hands at all, but in the hands of the producers.

On June 13, 1949—the day on which Dr. Hjalmar Schacht was cleared by a de-Nazification court in Stuttgart—the Court of Appeals for the District of Columbia, in a unanimous verdict written by Mr. Justice Clark, upheld the convictions in the following words:

Neither Congress nor any Court is required to disregard the impact of world events, however impartially or dispassionately they view them. It is equally beyond dispute that the motion picture industry plays a critically prominent role in the molding of public opinion and that motion pictures are, or are capable of being, a potent medium of propaganda dissemination which may influence the minds of millions of American people. This being so, it is absurd to argue, as these appellants do, that questions asked men who, by their authorship of the scripts, vitally influence the ultimate production of motion pictures seen by millions, which questions require disclosure of whether or not they are or ever have been Communists, are not pertinent questions.

The Court of Appeals has answered Mr. De Voto's admonition to the embattled universities with a clear verboten. The Court of Appeals holds that speech can be controlled whenever it relates to an important and vital matter or is expressed through an effective medium of communication. Freedom of speech is thereby reserved only for unimportant speech, ineffectively communicated. Since the instruction of youth is a vital matter and the profession of teaching an effective means of communication, the schools and universities of the country—by order of the court—must yield up not only their textbooks, but their instructors as well.

All effective communication upon any important subject—whether it occurs in a newspaper, the cinema, the radio, the theatre, the novel, the short story, the press, the laboratory, the pulpit, or the classroom—becomes, as of June 13, 1949, the legitimate object of government regulation.

Mr. John S. Wood of Georgia is now more important to the theatre than Mr. Arthur Miller, to nuclear physics than Dr. Albert Einstein, to education than Dr. James B. Conant.

The standards of the Toad have achieved the sanctity of written law.

* * *

What is it, then, which delivers the leaders of a great nation into such an excess of hysteria that they fear and actually assert their power to prohibit the utterance of any word which may be spoken in opposition to their purposes? What great designs must there be shrouded in darkness? What visions have disturbed the national dream to invoke this high and holy madness?

M. de Caulaincourt, Duke of Vicenza and general under the first Napoleon, relates in his memoirs a conversation he held with the Emperor at St. Cloud in 1811—the year in which that able tyrant was perfecting his plans for the conquest of Russia:

> The Emperor repeated all the fantastic stories which, to please him, were fabricated in Danzig, in the Duchy of Warsaw, and even in the north of Germany—stories the accuracy of which had been disproved time and again, sometimes by means of investigations carried out on the spot, sometimes even by the march of events.
>
> "Admit frankly," said the Emperor Napoleon, "that it is Alexander who wants to make war on me."
>
> "No, Sire," I replied once again, "I would stake my life on his not firing the first shot or being the first to cross his frontiers."

Napoleon obsessed with his great objective and unwilling to hear any word against it, later remarked in Caulaincourt's presence: "M. de Caulaincourt has turned Russian. The Tsar's beguilements have won him over." And then, speaking directly to Caulaincourt: "You have turned Russian, haven't you?"

To which the general replied, "I am a good Frenchman, Sire, and time will prove that I have told Your Majesty the truth, as a faithful servant should."

Time did prove it, when Caulaincourt accompanied his beaten Emperor in that famous personal retreat from Moscow and a starving army. Throughout the whole long journey Napoleon made no mention of their previous disagreement. He was too engrossed in savoring the destiny of men in whose ears the voice of moderation is always amplified to treason.

Mr. Archibald MacLeish in the *Atlantic Monthly* observes the same symptoms in America and diagnoses the national malaise in this way:

What is happening in the United States under the impact of the negative and defensive and often frightened opinion of these years is the falsification of the image the American people have long cherished of themselves as beginners and begetters, changers and challengers, creators and accomplishers. A people who have thought of themselves for a hundred and fifty years as having purposes of their own for the changing of the world cannot learn overnight to think of themselves as the resisters of another's purposes without beginning to wonder who they are. A people who have been real to themselves because they were for something cannot continue to be real to themselves when they find they are merely against something.

Although he arrives at a conclusion with which this writer is not in sympathy. Here Mr. MacLeish has reached the core of the matter. We are against the Soviet Union in our foreign policy abroad, and we are against anything partaking of socialism or Communism in our internal affairs. This quality of opposition has become the keystone of our national existence. With hatred of *their* society the only patriotic measure of devotion to our own, action gives way to reaction and initiative trails off to mere response. What our enemy does we must not do; what he does not we must at any cost do ourselves. Each morning we observe the drift of the wind out of the Don Basin. At lunch-time we test the temperature of the Siberian wilderness. At night we are canny with the moon, for it shines also upon the domes of Moscow.

If there be hurricanes in Florida we must discover more savage gales in the Crimea, for sunshine and citrus are to be found there, too, although of an inferior quality. If we keep fifteen million Negroes in desperate peonage, it is not so bad if only we can unearth twenty millions in Russia suffering a more brutal peonage—and white peons at that. If, by some evil chance, a two-headed monster is born to a Minnesota housewife, then we are obliged to make of it a virtue by proving that Russian mothers are compelled to beget two-headed monsters as a matter of national policy.

The Soviet Union has become a moral yardstick by which we evaluate our national deeds and virtues. We must commit no deed, large or small or good or bad, without first measuring it to the Soviet pattern. And if, in making our daily genuflections toward the

Kremlin, its towers are obscured by fog, we are paralyzed. We cannot move at all until the weather clears.

The attitude has developed into a full-blown cult, complete with hierarchy, prophets, and lay readers: the cult of the New Liberalism, or the "non-Communist left." No one in his right senses would wish to quarrel with any progressive political coalescence, for the forces to the left of center have been seriously weakened by four years of ferocious attack, and certainly recruits are to be desired. But the New Liberals have no stomach for liberalism itself, save on a high and almost theological plane. When the battle is actually joined on a specific issue involving the lives and rights of existing men—as in the recent case of the Trenton Six—they are not to be found in the lists. They abandon such earthy matters to organizations designated "subversive" by the attorney-general, meanwhile engaging their own energies in the production of spirited manifestos in support of the status quo antebellum, which is the furthermost limit of their aspirations.

The self-conscious label "non-Communist left," indicating more what the worshippers are not than what they are, is naturally reflected in cult policy. Any serious examination of the sacred writings of the "non-Communist left" reveals that it has, in fact, become the "non-anti-fascist left." Its collective zeal is expended not in being "non-Communist" but in a fight waged almost exclusively against Communists. The difference is not subtle. It transforms the whole spirit of the movement. Its dogma has become nine parts anti-Communism to one part anti-Toryism, or anti-reaction, or—comically enough—anti- anything but fascism. For fascism is the dirty word of the sect: it must not be used because it has been willed out of existence.

During a period when Communists, real or alleged or only suspected, are being prosecuted everywhere for their thoughts and speech and never for their acts, the "non-Communist left" has invoked a unique attack upon all who protest such obvious violations of civil rights. "Would you," they demand, "protest so loudly if the victims were fascists?"—thus beclouding the fact that except for the fascist Terminiello, who was freed by the Supreme Court on the grounds that his right of free speech had been violated, there is no single instance in the country today of a fascist being hauled before any tribunal to account for his thoughts or speech, or even being seriously prosecuted for the commission of such actual crimes as lynching, flogging, and arson. By equating Communism with fascism they bring to mind that other "non-Communist left" which on May 17, 1933 gave a unanimous vote of confidence to Hitler's foreign policy—and four weeks later found itself outlawed by the policy it had endorsed.

The New Liberals are fondest of citing the Nazi-Soviet non-aggression pact of August 23, 1939 as authority for a doctrine formerly subscribed to only by Mr. William Randolph Hearst and his peers. But search through their holy writings as you may, you will find no mention of the French-Italian agreement of January 7, 1935; the Anglo-Nazi Naval treaty of June 18, 1935; the British-Italian accord of April 16, 1938; the Munich pact of September 29, 1938; the Anglo-Nazi non-aggression pact of September 30, 1938; or the French-Nazi non-aggression pact of December 6, 1938—all of which preceded and considerably affected the one pact they cherish and recall.

Neither do they mention the fact that Roosevelt, Churchill, and Stalin at Yalta pledged themselves to "wipe out the Nazi party, Nazi laws, organizations and institutions, remove all Nazi and militarist influence from public office and from the cultural and economic life of the German people." For the liberated areas they pledged themselves to "processes which will enable the liberated peoples to destroy the last vestiges of Nazism and Fascism." At the opposite end of the pole they pledged that "all democratic and anti-Nazi parties" including quite naturally the Communist "shall have the right to take part and to put forward candidates." The leaders of the democratic coalition did not equate fascism with Communism.

If the New Liberals really believe the doctrine they put forth, they must equate the racial mystique of Nietzsche, Houston Stewart Chamberlain, Hitler, Rosenberg, and Goebbels with the writings of Marx, Engels, Lenin, and Stalin. They must equate 6,000,000 Jews burned and gassed and tortured to death in the territories of Nazi Germany with 3,500,000 Jews living in the Soviet Union under the protection of laws which ban discrimination of any kind.[14] They must equate the slogans "Blut und boden" or "Ein Volk, ein Reich, ein Fuehrer" with the slogan "From each according to his ability, to each according to his work." It is quite possible to disagree with each factor of every equation; but reasonable men simply cannot maintain they are the same.

Thus the New Liberals are deflected by the holy sickness from any effective attack upon what I am sure they call the "non-fascist right," and have become even more ardent in their genuflections toward Moscow than the State Department itself. To illustrate by one of a hundred quotes: "The slums of America are breeding spots of Communism, and in passing this (housing) legislation we will be striking a blow against Socialism and Communism and for our free enterprise system and our American democracy."

Eliminate the slums because they are indecent and unjust? Because they spawn disease and torment and illiteracy and death? No. Eliminate them because they breed Communism. We do not accomplish the good deed for itself; we do it as an act of war forced upon us by an implacable enemy. And without Communism, one is tempted to ask—what then? Since no moral purpose impels us to slum-clearance, we would take no action if the menace of Communism did not exist. But, one asks, if slums are of themselves rotten,

14. Which, in afterthought, were not and are not obeyed. —D.T.

and if it is the pressure of Communism which obliges us to eliminate this rot—what then becomes the role of Communism in such a system of logic? It becomes the role of virtue; the catalytic agent through which progress is accomplished; the enzyme without which no improvement is possible. It becomes, by the speaker's own reasoning, a very good thing. This is not what the speaker means, for he hates Communism. But it is what he said.

How different the voice of President Roosevelt, who was not afflicted with such holy madness:

> There are those who say there is no answer, that this great city and all great cities must hide in dark alleyways and dingy street buildings that disgrace our modern civilization; where disease follows poverty and crime follows both. . . . I believe you will take this up as a body, in mutual confidence, and apply your most practical knowledge to this matter of housing our poor.

Or that even greater moment when he said:

> I see one-third of a nation ill-housed, ill-clad, ill-nourished. It is not in despair that I paint you that picture. I paint it for you in hope—because the nation, seeing and understanding the injustice of it, proposes to paint it out.

There spoke the voice, as Mr. MacLeish puts it, of "beginners and begetters, changers and challengers, creators and accomplishers." The voice of a people moving with sanity toward a moral objective, not to win strategic advantage in a cold war, but to exalt the dignity of man.

Even so distinguished a woman as Mrs. Eleanor Roosevelt falls victim now and again to the current fevers. She writes of the Peekskill riots:

> One hundred forty-five persons were injured, fifty busses were stoned, and a number of private cars, many of which did not contain people who had been at this concert, were molested and damaged. This is not the type of thing that we believe in in the United States. If peaceful picketing leads to this, all the pickets do is to give the Communists good materials for propaganda. . . . I was particularly sorry to hear that one of the busses and a number of cars which were man-handled by a particular group that was not controlled by the police authorities were cars that were returning from the Hyde Park Memorial Library and held people who had not been to the Robeson concert.

Mrs. Roosevelt, who has complained in her column that America's treatment of Negroes provides fuel for Communist propaganda and adds difficulties to her work on the Human Rights Commission of the United Nations, goes on to say that: ". . . if he (Mr. Robeson) wants to give a concert or speak his mind in public, no one should prevent him from doing so."

But this is not enough. She has already made the fatal concession to Mr. De Voto's principle of the "partial virgin." She is "particularly" sorry that visitors to Hyde Park were molested, along with others who had not been to the concert. She disapproves molestation of her friends a little more than of those with whom she is not in agreement. Her friends partake of the nature of innocence, and those with whom she disagrees of guilt, and she is led by her dislike to an implicit disavowal of the Bill of Rights. She does not mean it so, but that is what she says.

By saying it she permits Miss Hedda Hopper to crawl into the fatal breach there left unguarded, and tell her readers in the *Los Angeles Times:* "Paul Robeson will appear at Wrigley Field September 30. I must say he's giving our people plenty of time to heat up a reception." Thus a leading citizen of the world becomes linked—however wide the degree of difference—by careless thinking and a mutual enemy, to a common purveyor of small adulteries.

If the best and noblest among us falls victim to this malady, it is not surprising that lesser men hasten to proclaim their infection. Thus the mayor of Los Angeles, his chief of police indicted for perjury, his leading detectives torn between bribery and extortion, his city overrun with gangsters, announces valid reason for a cleanup:

> Nothing is more welcomed by Communists and the subversive elements of our population than to see mistrust of government, confusion, disturbance, and hoodlums, racketeers and those who make crime their principal business profit, and the public interest suffer.

For a parallel one is obliged to go back to Alphonse Capone eighteen years before the District Court of Appeals wrote his views into law:

> Bolshevism is knocking at our gates. We can't afford to let it in. We have got to organize ourselves against it, and

put our shoulders to the wheel together and hold fast. We must keep the worker away from red literature and red ruses; we must see that his mind remains healthy.

Sometimes the inflamed grenadiers of the cold war, even though moving toward a common goal, break the line of march to stab a laggard, as when Mr. Arthur M. Schlesinger, Jr., defending "The Right to Loathsome Ideas" among university personnel, ran afoul of Mr. Morris Ernst.

From the chilly heights of three years at Harvard, where he holds an associate professorship in the department in which his father occupies the Francis Lee Higginson chair of history, Mr. Schlesinger hurled the epithet "wretched nonentities" at three University of Washington professors who, combining sixty-six years of university teaching in their total experience, had been discharged—two for stating they were Communists, one for saying he had been.

Deploring the fact that the discharged men are "far more powerful in martyrdom than they were in freedom," and denouncing them as "contemptible individuals who have deliberately lived a political lie"—although it was their statement of the truth which proved their undoing—Mr. Schlesinger arrived at the tortuous conclusion that, "No university administration in its right senses would knowingly hire a Communist. . . . But, once given academic tenure, none of these can properly be fired on the basis of beliefs alone short of clear and present danger."

Mr. Ernst, perceiving the flaws of the argument, hastened to point out that the moral right to refuse to hire a scoundrel also carries with it the obligation to fire him, no matter how long he has browsed in the academic pasture. As for Mr. Schlesinger's theory of free speech in relation to clear and present danger, Mr. Ernst developed a totally new concept of speech. He distinguished between free speech as commonly practiced, and "secret speech" as practiced by Communists. The latter variety, he asserted, carries with it no immunities whatever.

Mr. Louis Russell, investigator for the Un-American Activities Commitee and an avid reader of the *Daily Worker*, the *People's World*, *Masses and Mainstream,* and *Political Affairs,* would be perplexed at Mr. Ernst's ideas about the "secrecy" of such speech. But he would agree with his conclusions, as one day Mr. Schlesinger will too, if he hasn't already; for they are all possessed, in only varying degrees, of the same affliction.

Nowhere does the epidemic rage more fiercely than among the publicists and critics and space-rate Cains who infest the half-world of the semi-slick reviews. No approach may be made to any American work without evaluating it, for better or worse, against its Soviet counterpart, or estimating its effectiveness in the cold war.

Mr. John Gunther is reproved in the pages of the *Saturday Review of Literature* for his own reproval of Mr. Ernest Bevin, who called Premier Stalin and Marshal Tito "thugs." The reviewer of *Behind the Iron Curtain* pointed out that they are thugs, and in times like ours one must call a thug a thug. Mr. Clifton Fadiman, same magazine, worries about something called "the decline of attention," attributing it to "a wholesale displacement away from ideas and abstractions toward things and techniques." And who is to blame? "The movement toward displacement is the result of calculated policy in such police states as the Soviet Union." Mr. Elmer Davis, *Saturday Review* again, in passing on to a larger subject, and without any supporting evidence, refers to the "defenestration" of Mr. Jan Masaryk without a thought in his innocent mind of the death of Mr. James Forrestal. There is scarcely enough toad-meat to go around.

Where amidst this "formidable army of sychophants and delators" can be heard even the whisper of reason? Who in these frightened ranks has ever stopped to ask himself: Is this after all a matter of the intellect, an affair of some philosophic substance, a question not entirely to be resolved by incantation? Has any one of them heard above the din from Brocken the voice of Thomas Mann declaring that

> I testify, moreover, that to my mind the ignorant and superstitious persecution of the believers in a political and economic doctrine which is, after all, the creation of great minds and great thinkers—I testify that this persecution is not only degrading for the persecutors themselves but also very harmful to the cultural reputation of this country?

No. That voice was not heard. The holy sickness not only maddens its victims; it deafens them as well.

These men who might have been the bravest and best loved, these soldiers of the intellect to whom a troubled people looks for truth, have abandoned the outposts of reason like unfaithful sentries in the night. Hand in hand and chanting tribal hymns they have deserted into the land of Chaos. There they sit in perpetual twilight, confuting folly with unreason, muttering like frightened murshids of the mystery and menace of the Slavic soul. There they build their fires before the ancient totems and prepare to offer up in living sacrifice the mind of a generation.

* * *

At the conclusion of the Hollywood hearings on October 31, 1937, the indicted ten again purchased newspaper space to declare: "Not only a free screen, but every free institution in America is jeopardized as long as this committee exists. . . . Our original determination to abolish the committee remains unchanged." They also took this last opportunity to warn the country that "education, atomic energy and trade unions are the next targets" of the committee.

How goes the matter two years later? How goes the loyalty check—that iniquitous process which inquires of men whether they associate with Jews or Negroes, what magazines they read, what candidates they vote for, what meetings they attend?

It goes well. The city of Washington is a city of whispers, of tapped phones and cautious meetings; a city whose very air is polluted with the smell of the secret police. "There are political forces so manipulating things on Capitol Hill today," writes Roscoe Drummond, Washington bureau chief of the *Christian Science Monitor,*

> that Congress is being put in a position of being so almost totally concerned with exposing and condemning the activities of Communism in the United States that it is almost totally unconcerned with exposing and condemning the activities of fascism in the United States. . . . This isn't protection of democracy at all; this is imperiling democracy. . . . There are so many evidences of Congressional preoccupation with the dangers of Communism to democracy and Congressional indifference to the threats of fascism to democracy that they no longer can be dismissed as casual or unintentional. They appear deliberate and purposeful.

From the postal services of outlying cities there come occasional reports, cautious and confidential and never complete. They read like casualty lists from a battleground, as indeed they are: Of 34 persons known to have been purged in Cleveland, 24 were Negroes and four were Jews. Of 41 known to have been discharged in Philadelphia, 12 were Negroes and 21 were Jews. Of 14 known to have been fired in Los Angeles, 12 were Negroes and one was an American of Mexican origin. Of 133 known to have been fired throughout the country, 72 were Negroes and 48 were Jews.

This is not surprising. Anti-Semitism and Negrophobia among Federal bureaucrats is well known and never mentioned. With the policy-makers of such Neanderthalic cast it is only reasonable that purge lists should reflect their distaste. When they address the world upon matters affecting the lives and fortunes of millions, or when they weep in public for the oppressed and downtrodden of other countries, it is well to remember that the voice is Democratia's voice, but the hands are the hands of the Toad. The purges go well.

How goes Congressional censorship of motion pictures? It goes excellently. The Committee on Un-American Activities called for the discharge of ten men on political grounds. The motion picture monopoly promptly broke all existing contracts with the accused men and, in theory at least, banned them for life from the practice of their profession. Beyond the blacklisted ten there extends a vague and shadowy "gray list" composed of scores of men and women whose ideas and politics might possibly give offense to the committee. And beyond the gray list lies a wide and spreading area of general fear in which unconventional ideas or unpopular thoughts are carefully concealed by self-censorship.

The committee did not only tell the producers whom they might not employ: it also told them what kind of pictures they must make in the future. Throughout the hearings the committee demanded over and again why anti-Communist pictures were not being made and when they would be made.[15] The

15. "Under those circumstances, I would like to know whether or not Warner Brothers has made, or is making at the present time, any pictures pointing out the methods and the

producers returned to their studios and immediately set about the production of the films for which the committee had called. *The Iron Curtain, I Married a Communist, The Red Menace, The Red Danube* and *Guilty of Treason*—all of them calculated to provoke hatred and incite to war—were made without reference to audience demand, possible profit, or normal entertainment value. They were produced as the direct result of Congressional command over the content of American motion pictures.

Even though it is customary in intellectual circles to deplore motion pictures as an art, it would be a fatal mistake to underestimate them as an influence. They constitute perhaps the most important medium for the communication of ideas in the world today. The Committee on Un-American Activities recognizes them as such. The Circuit Court of Appeals recognizes them as such. The Legion of Decency and the National Association of Manufacturers and the American Legion and the National Chamber of Commerce recognize them as such. Unless intellectuals quickly come to the same conclusion and act as vigorously as

---

evils of totalitarian communism, as you so effectively have pointed out the evils of the totalitarian Nazis."—Mr. Richard Nixon to Mr. Jack Warner, HUAC Hollywood Hearings, October 20, 1947, p. 28.

"Under the circumstances, I think this committee is glad to hear that Warner Brothers is contemplating for the first time now making a motion picture in which they point out to the American people the dangers of totalitarian communism as well as fascism."—Mr. Richard Nixon to Mr. Jack Warner, *Ibid.*, p. 29.

their enemies, there is an excellent chance that the American motion picture monopoly, abasing itself as the German monopoly did, will succeed in its assigned task of preparing the minds of its audiences for the violence and brutality and perverted morality which is fascism.

How goes the encroachment of politics upon science? It goes very well. Scholarships have been restricted to the elite; the Congress has asserted its power over atomic decisions; the president has complained that the committee on Un-American Activities renders it difficult to find competent personnel; the Federation of Atomic Scientists has been all but silenced; the conspiracy between the military and the banks to surrender the incalculable riches of atomic energy into private hands progresses nicely.

Mr. De Voto declares:

> There is a growing suspicion, which a lot of us would like aired, that the generals and admirals are demanding and being accorded the right to determine the political (and what others?) opinions of the scientists whose salaries they are paying. If they are not making that demand now, we can be quite sure they will be tomorrow.

Dr. Edward U. Condon, head of the United States Bureau of Standards, reveals that one of the charges made against him was that "you have been highly critical of the older ideas in physics," and goes on to warn that "anti-intellectualism precedes the totalitarian pusch, and anti-intellectualism is on the upswing here."

How goes the infliction of censorship upon art? It goes well. Representative George A. Dondero of Michigan has addressed Congress to the extent of ten columns in the Congressional Record on the subject of "Communism in the Heart of American Art—What to Do About It." Mr. Dondero was inflamed by a Gallery on Wheels—an art exhibit for the benefit of the men in veterans hospitals, to which twenty-eight artists had contributed their work.

The Congressman cited fifteen of the artists as Communists or sympathizers, and went into the political records of thirteen of them. Important among the charges he made was support of Mr. Henry A. Wallace's candidacy. Declaring that "the art of the Communist and the Marxist is the art of perversion," he denounced the contributors as ". . . radicals all . . . explaining their theories to an audience who could not get away from them. . . . They had a great opportunity not only to spread propaganda, but to engage in espionage." One important art gallery also came under Mr. Dondero's fire, which culminated in a demand for "a major investigation on the part of a competent governmental agency" and, while disavowing any intent of censorship, demanded "directional supervision" of art critics by their superiors.

Mr. Arthur Miller, art editor of the *Los Angeles Times* states that the Congressman's attacks "have resulted in the return of paintings by named artists to New York art dealers, the loss of a mural commission and the expulsion of at least one well-known artist, a National Academician, from a conservative artists' club." He also reports that "the reviews of one New York critic, respected by her colleagues, are reportedly being personally edited by her publisher. . . ."

Presumably the baiting of modern American art would not trouble President Truman, who has participated in the sport himself; nor the State Department which, under Secretary Marshall, abjectly withdrew its traveling show of modern American artists at the first breath of "conservative" criticism and sold it as war surplus.

How goes the campaign against free inquiry in schools and universities? It goes extremely well. The roll call of professors purged during 1948: Dr. Clarence R. Athern, professor of philosophy and social ethics, Lycoming College; Professor Daniel D. Ashkenas, University of Miami; Professor James Barfoot, University of Georgia; Professor Lyman R. Bradley, head of the German department, New York University; Professor Joseph Butterworth, associate in English, University of Washington; Professor Leonard Cohen, Jr., University of Miami; Professor Charles G. Davis, University of Miami; Professor Ralph H. Gundlach, associate in psychology, University of Washington; Dr. Richard G. Morgan, Curator of the Ohio State Museum; Mr. Clyde Miller of Teachers College, Columbia University; Professor Luther K. McNair, Dean of Lyndon State Teachers College; Professor Herbert J. Phillips, assistant in philosophy, University of Washington; Dr. George Parker, professor of Bible and philosophy, Methodist Evansville College; Professor Ralph Spitzer, University of Oregon, Professor Don West of Oglethorpe.

Charges against these men ranged from stating under oath they were Communists and being in contempt of the Committee on Un-American Activities to supporting Mr. Wallace for the presidency and running for the governorship of Georgia.

But the formal leaders of American education have gone even farther toward restricting academic freedom. They have resolved to save their house from the arsonists of the Un-American Activities committee by setting fire to it themselves. In the recent report of the National Educational Association and the American Association of School Administrators—a synopsis of which was overwhelmingly approved at the NEA convention—they have not only barred Communists from their faculties; they have thoughtfully handed down a plan for a complete renovation of the American mind.

The report was predicated upon the assumption that "the cold war will continue for many years" and therefore requires a "basic psychological reorientation for the American people as a whole." Admitting that "it is deeply patriotic to attempt to protect one's country and one's fellow citizens from the calamities of war" it nevertheless points out that "in the years just ahead it will not always be easy to teach such things as these in American schools." However "the schools of the United States will certainly be expected and required to continue their work in developing strong individual national loyalties" which inevitably will reveal "the need for healthy young people to wear uniforms and man machines. . . ." The report exhorts educators to work toward that time when education shall deserve to receive popular support "as an instrument of national policy."

Education, hitherto presumed to consist of free inquiry into the nature of truth, thus becomes merely an instrument of whatever policy the nation momentarily may pursue. That policy, determined outside the university and being on its own *ipse dixit* right, obviously cannot be subject to free inquiry. When policy has been made, inquiry ceases. National policy is truth, truth is national policy. It cannot be otherwise.

The report was signed by twenty leading educators, among them that politico-military pedagogue, General Dwight D. Eisenhower, and Dr. James B. Conant of Harvard, who immediately afterward found himself in a preposterous situation when the author of the Maryland Loyalty Bills—later declared unconstitutional—demanded that since Dr. Conant had pledged himself to bar Communists from the university in the future, he discharge those already employed. Dr. Conant replied with a resounding peroration against faculty witch hunts, but logic did not abide with him. He retired to the same corner into which Mr. Ernst knocked Mr. Schlesinger, there to receive unguents from the partial virgin who has made of that place her domain.

We have retreated almost the full distance from President Roosevelt's "No group and no government can properly prescribe precisely what should constitute the body of knowledge with which true education is concerned. The truth is found where men are free to pursue it" to William Jennings Bryan's "No teacher should be allowed on the faculty of any American University unless he is a Christian."

There are, however, still men in the academic world who speak out bravely. Dr. Robert B. Pettengill of the Teaching Institute of Economics, University of Southern California, writes in the *Los Angeles Times:*

> The fear of being accused of heresy causes professors to lean over backward to avoid teaching anything which might make them suspect. Impartiality is no longer safe. Partisanship on the 'right' side is the way to gain promotion. And those in the pay of approved groups or dependent upon their favor will continue as now to violate the standards of free industry and free teaching in the name of which you would purge Communists.

Dr. Robert M. Hutchins, chancellor of the University of Chicago, carried the issue boldly to the Illinois Subversive Activities Commission. Pressed to admit that Communists were traitors upon the evidence that President Truman had called them such, Dr. Hutchins replied: "You will forgive me for saying there is reason why we should not model our vocabularies on the President's." While expressing his opposition to Communism, he went on to say that

> The University of Chicago does not believe in the doctrine of guilt by association. . . . As is well known, there is a Communist club among the students of the university. Eleven students belong to it. The club has not sought to subvert the government of this state. Its members claim they are interested in studying Communism, and some of them, perhaps all of them, may be sympathetic towards Communism. But the study of Communism is not a subversive activity.

Professor Dwight E. Dumond of the University of Michigan concludes:

> What we must say is: that until every Teachers' Oath law is repealed; and every Board of Regents is told that it cannot interfere with the inalienable rights of free discussion by faculty and students, in the classroom and out, on the campus and off, . . . man's eternal fight for freedom is dangerously compromised.

Mr. Dumond does not speak only for himself. In those universities where freedom of academic opinion is an established custom, educators are speaking out boldly. When the Board of Regents of the University of California recently prescribed a non-Communist oath, the faculty academic senate at Berkeley, according to the U.C.L.A. *Bruin,* rejected the proposal by a vote of "approximately 700 to one," while the same body of the university in Los Angeles voted a unanimous no. The issue still remains to be fought out, but at the University of California it does not go by default.

Mr. De Voto understands such matters. He is no Communist. He is not sympathetic to Communism. He is, if I read his *Harper's* article right, a convinced opponent of Communism and a formidable one. But he understands a fight and he is hopelessly addicted to logic. Speaking of those university heads who, announcing their intention to resist inquisition, simultaneously agreed to ban Communists, he says:

> they have already lost the battle of the outposts, and have lost it by voluntarily retreating from a position of great strength. . . . If a college is to protect the freedom by which alone it exists in the tradition of democratic education, it has got to run the risk. The full risk.

And the full risk, adds Mr. De Voto, is allowing Communists on the faculty.

There is, indeed, no other stand to be made. Either the fight is carried forward without compromise—in the civil services, in private industry, in the arts, the sciences, the church, the universities—or it will not effectively be made at all. The pastel feints of a Conant or a Schlesinger, illogical as a flight of fleas, are worse than no fight at all. They are mere quarrels, always attended by disaster, and their creamy contradictions bring embarrassment to those who must clean up the mess.

The fight has already begun. It has been going on for two years. As of today it goes badly. If you are engaged in any work which may be interpreted by any

Congressman as dealing with the "molding of public opinion"; if you are involved with anything which is —or is capable of being—"a potent medium of propaganda," or which can "influence the minds of millions"; or if by "authorship" you "vitally influence" anything which may be "seen by millions," you are subject to every compulsion he may wish to put upon you.

That is the law as it stands in the case of the Hollywood Ten. It is the law as it applies to you. Only the Supreme Court can reverse this judgment. The Court has been tragically ravaged by the death of two of its ablest members, Justices Murphy and Rutledge. It is a Court the temper of which may have changed materially in the past two months.

While it is true, as Mr. William Seagle remarks in his *Men of Law,* that "A man cannot change a lifetime of habits of partisanship by taking the judicial oath. The past is always an entangling alliance."—what Justice Oliver Wendell Holmes said is also true:

The felt necessities of the times, the prevalent moral and political theories, intuitions of public policy, avowed or unconscious, even the prejudices which judges share with their fellow men, have had a good deal more to do than the syllogism in determining the rules by which men should be governed.

If the fight is to be won we must therefore change "the prevalent moral and political theories" and the "intuitions of public policy" which may influence the Court. Here is a task which calls for more than stately memoranda or measured speech unheard beyond the cloister. It calls for crying out in the streets. We are witnessing the murder of a tradition, and when murder is going on it is more honorable to jostle angrily in public than to appear as witness at the inquest.

Franklin Delano Roosevelt would have thundered out against the treachery afoot and destroyed it. Those around him would have thundered too. But not the least among the late president's talents was his remarkable ability to make his associates appear to be men—a piece of wizardry no one has been able to bring off since. Those who were men in their own right still remain what they were. Mr. Henry Wallace, Mr. Harold L. Ickes, Dr. Rexford Guy Tugwell, Mr. Archibald MacLeish—these and certain others, while differing among themselves, have not felt obliged to repudiate those principles which animated their services to the Roosevelt administration. But most of the late president's companions, deprived of courage and even of identity by his death, hang on in a pitiable state of suspension, "half indoors, half out of doors," sniffing every breeze that blows and unwilling to fight for anything but their share of the toad.

We shall have to do without these plastic warriors in the campaign ahead. We shall have to depend upon our ability to summon from its slumber the immense devotion to Constitutional government which still abides with the American people. We shall have to reassert the dignity of the intellect. We shall have to reestablish the pleasures of reason. And in the course of it we shall have to rescue those partial virgins of the mind from the low resorts into which they have fallen and restore them to the house of their fathers.

It can be done. There are resolute men and women in the arts, the sciences, the professions, and the clergy if only they be heard; and there are determined men and women by the millions outside. The moral climate of a nation can be changed overnight if the crisis be great enough, the will strong, the truth known.

But if it should occur in this battle of the mind against encroaching and oppressive law that an occasional Communist appears upon the lists, he must be defended too. Not with the high-piping invective of a Schlesinger, not while calling him a scoundrel worthy of hell's own damnation, for if you defend him in this manner your case is fatally weakened. If, because of the political labels attached to men, you have lost all capacity to judge them by their words and acts; if, in brief, you believe a Communist to be a scoundrel per se, then you cannot defend him. But by the bitter necessities of history and of logic, neither can you defend yourself.

Adolph Hitler said: "Bismark told us that liberalism was the pace-maker of Social Democracy. I need not say here that Social Democracy is the pace-maker of Communism." Similarly Mr. J. Parnell Thomas equates "New Dealism" with Communism.

The legal principles which protect one against the force of the state protect all. If a Communist comes first under attack and is overwhelmed, the breach opened by his fall becomes an avenue for the advance of the enemy with all his increased prestige upon you. You need not agree with the Communist while you engage in his and your common defense. You may, indeed, oppose him with every honorable weapon in your arsenal, dissociate yourself from his theories and repudiate his final objectives. But defend him you must, for his defeat in the Constitutional battle involves the overturn of principles which thus far have stood as our principal barrier, short of bloodshed, against fascism.

The case of the Hollywood Ten is not the first instance of a challenge offered to the Committee on Un-American Activities. Mr. Eugene Dennis, General Secretary of the Communist Party; Mr. Richard Morford of the Society for American-Soviet Friendship; Mr. George Marshall of the National Federation for Constitutional Liberties; the directors of the Joint Anti-Fascist Refugee Committee—these and others have vigorously challenged the power of the committee on half a dozen fronts. Without exception the men involved have suffered conviction, and now rest their cases on appeal before the Supreme Court. There has not yet been a single victory over the committee in the courts.

How to cry havoc and yet not spread despair? It would be a damaging overstatement to contend that the case of the Hollywood Ten is the ultimate battle—although the decision of the court is sweeping enough to tempt such a conclusion—or that all depends upon the outcome. The forces of repression have almost the endurance of those of progress, and the contest between them will extend into the remotest future. But there are landmarks; there are occasions when one side has gained a decisive advantage, compelling the loser to toil for weary years to regain a position even of competitive equality.

It is no exaggeration to say that the case of the Ten represents such a landmark. It is a direct challenge to the censorial power of government over the human mind. If it is lost, the customary rights of free speech —provided the government chooses to use the power bestowed upon it, and governments rarely seek power for idle purposes—may legally be abrogated. If it is won, then the sinister twins of compulsory confession and political censorship will, at the very least, have been stunned; not forever certainly, but long enough to give free men respite and time to marshal their energies. The case is the immediate outpost in a long line of battle. If it holds, all will hold, and even advance a little. If it falls, all will share in the defeat and in the hard years of struggle to make up for it.

The issue being thus clearly joined, all who profess interest in the preservation of Constitutional procedure must accept the materials with which they have been presented—the Committee on Un-American Activities on the one hand and the Hollywood Ten on the other—and enter into the conflict as conscience dictates. Whether they enter or not, they will be considerably affected by the outcome, and it is generally accounted desirable to have a hand in one's own fate.

* * * *

Afternote

On April 10, 1950, the Supreme Court denied certiorari in the cases of John Howard Lawson and Dalton Trumbo (which governed the cases of all ten), and on May 29 denied a petition for rehearing, Justices Black and Douglas dissenting in both decisions.

In response to a defense plea that incarceration in California's or Arizona's five Federal prison facilities would facilitate visits from wives and twenty-three children, the Federal Bureau of Prisons dispatched two of the men to Danbury, Connecticut; three to Ashland, Kentucky; two to Millpoint, West Virginia; and two to Texarkana, Texas. Samuel Ornitz, who was in failing health, served his sentence at the Federal Medical Center in Springfield, Missouri.

Once behind bars, the contemnees immediately addressed themselves to problems of parole. If it can be granted that eligibility for parole ought in some degree to call for contrite hearts and resolutions to sin no more, their routine appearances before representatives of the Parole Board must have been as confusing to both sides as all that had gone before.

Applications denied, the prisoners served their full terms and were released in 1951.

There followed a slow adjustment to new and different circustances, a diaspora of sorts, which endured for years—New York, London, Paris, Mexico City—and then a gradual return to where it had all begun. Two of them are now dead; one lives in New York; seven in California.

The Ten

Alvah Bessie has published *Inquisition in Eden,* an autobiographical account of the blacklist period, and a novel entitled *The Symbol.* He appeared as an actor in the Spanish production of *Spain Again,* which was based on his novel of the same title. He contributes regularly to cultural and film reviews on both sides of the Atlantic. He lives in Terra Linda, California.

Herbert Biberman published *Salt of the Earth,* an account of difficulties attendant on the production of his celebrated film of the same name. His last motion picture was *Slaves.* He died in 1971. His widow, Gale Sondergaard Biberman, lives in Los Angeles.

Lester Cole has turned to work in the European theatre. Of his plays, *The Obscene Temple* was produced in Prague; *Mistress of Mordasov* (from Dostoevski's *My Uncle's Dream*) and *Say Uncle* in England; and *Potiphar's House* (written with Alan Max) in Germany. He has lectured on film writing at the University of San Francisco. His last film was *Born Free*. He lives in San Francisco.

Edward Dmytryk appeared before the House Committee as a friendly witness after his release from jail, gave names, and has worked as a film director ever since. He is presently in Europe.

Ring Lardner, Jr. has published a novel, *The Ecstasy of Owen Muir*, and collaborated with Ian Hunter on the Broadway musical *Foxy*. He received an Academy Award in 1970 for his screenplay of *M*A*S*H*, which later won the Grand Prix at Cannes. He lives in New York City.

John Howard Lawson has published *The Hidden Heritage* and *Film: The Creative Process*. He has given courses at the Hebrew University and at Loyola College in Los Angeles, and he lectures widely on the social and aesthetic problems of film. Presently writing his autobiography, he lives in Los Angeles.

Albert Maltz had published two novels, *A Long Day in a Short Life* and *A Take of one January*, and a volume of short stories entitled *Afternoon in the Jungle*. His latest film is *Two Mules for Sister Sarah*. He lives in Los Angeles.

Samuel Ornitz published *Bride of the Sabbath*, the first novel of a trilogy that was interrupted in 1957 by his death. His widow, Mrs. Sadie Ornitz, lives in Los Angeles.

Adrian Scott worked in London as a production executive for Metro-Goldwyn-Mayer and other film companies. Since returning to the United States he has also written a number of network television shows. His most recent work as producer, a television film special for Universal-International entitled *The Great Man's Whiskers*, has not yet been released. He lives in Los Angeles.

Dalton Trumbo has published *Additional Dialogue: Letters of Dalton Trumbo, 1942–1962* and the present volume, *The Time of the Toad.* His latest film is *Johnny Got His Gun*, which he wrote and directed from his novel of the same name. It won the *Grand Prix Special du Jury* and International Critics Award at the 1971 Cannes Film Festival and the Audience and Directors, Writers and Technicians Awards as Best of Festival in Belgrade, 1972. He lives in Los Angeles.

The Devil in the Book

THE SMITH ACT

THE ALIEN REGISTRATION ACT of 1940, as passed by the Congress in that year, aroused only nominal opposition. War against the Axis powers was imminent and the new law was generally accepted as a regrettable but necessary device for curbing the activities of enemy aliens and fascist spies during the perilous years to come. As administered, however, the law had a somewhat different effect. Zechariah Chafee, Jr., of the Harvard Law School later wrote of it: "Hundreds of Communist workmen have been rounded up by immigration officials and deported. So far as I can ascertain, not one Nazi and not one Fascist has been arrested and shipped overseas."

Attached to the 1940 registration law was an obscure amendment called the Smith Amendment—later to become known as the Smith Act—which enacted into legal statute provisions for regulating, suppressing, and punishing any speech which was deemed a conspiracy to teach or advocate the overthrow of the

First published as a pamphlet in 1956.

government by force and violence. Its author was Howard W. Smith, whose intellect and devotion to constitutional principles may be judged by his recent presentation before the House of Representatives of the "Southern Manifesto" against desegregation.

Like the Alien Registration Law of which it was a part, the Smith Amendment was never really intended for use against fascists even in time of war. It was aimed not against the right but against the left and has consistently been so used. Just as legislation against fascists is almost always used against Communists, the prosecution of Communists inevitably imposes sanctions upon the activities and speech of millions of persons who, inimical though they may be to Communism, nonetheless struggle in specific areas for social objectives which both liberals and Communists desire.

The Smith Act has thus become the hallmark of a decade of repression and restriction not only of Communists but of the entire national community. The means by which Communists are imprisoned therefore becomes the concern of the whole people, since it is their liberty which is diminished by each conviction under the act.

For the purposes of these notes, the conviction of the fourteen California Smith Act defendants has been taken as a typical case. The quality of the defendants in all trials is approximately the same; the theory of the prosecution is the same; and above all else those dozens and dozens of books stacked on the table of the U.S. District Attorney—books which the government asserts to be the habitation of all manner of heretical devils—are invariably the same books.

In addition to its typicality, a further reason for selecting the California Smith Act trial lies in its untypicality: it is the first such case since the original Dennis decision which the United States Supreme Court has deemed to involve such substantial questions of law as to be worthy of the Court's review.

THE DEFENDANTS

There are fourteen convicted defendants in the California case. All of them are or have in the past been public officials of the Communist Party, in which capacity they have openly and vigorously professed their political views through every medium of communication open to them. They are not private and secret persons: they are public and voluble.

They are persons in the lower economic brackets, earning an average income of perhaps fifty dollars per week. Whatever crimes they are alleged to have committed were not done for money. Three of them are veterans of World War II, and one is a veteran of World War I. Four of them are women, and three of the women are mothers. They are the fathers and mothers of twenty children.

No violence of any kind has been charged against them. No illegal thing was found in their possession. No property was stolen by them, no door was forced, no purse was rifled. They cheated no one by the sale of worthless securities, stole no funds, collected no usury, evaded no taxes. No man was lynched at their hands, nor was any racial or national or religious minority humiliated or degraded by their words. No woman's body was sold by them or to them in prostitution, they instructed no youth in the use of drugs, and no child lay maimed or dead in the street for their carelessness.

What they actually have done and said may be found in the public press, in their political speeches and campaigns, in hundreds of leaflets they have distributed in thousand of copies, in the record of their political conventions, in the constitution of their party, and in their theoretical organ which is called *Political Affairs*.

They are vigorous proponents of active trade unionism, in which they view racial and sexual equality and united political action as essential to the successful struggle of American workers to better their economic condition. They advocate a comprehensive federal health program, increased social security coverage and benefits, a broad program of federal housing, and a federal fine arts department such as most civilized countries have had for decades. Many of the social reforms first advocated by the Communist Party have since been enacted into the legal structure of our government. In this sense, at least, the majority of Americans may be said to have approved and supported certain parts of the Communist program.

From the very inception of their party they have participated in the continuing struggle of the Negro people. While the main force in the drive for equality has always sprung from the Negro people themselves, Communists and these fourteen defendants have either initiated or participated in widespread campaigns for fair employment laws, desegregation of the public schools, outlawing of restrictive covenants, abolition of the poll tax, federal intervention in the murder and lynching of Negro citizens.

They have likewise organized massive protest against legal lynching as epitomized in the cases of the Scottsboro Boys, Willie McGee, the Martinsville Seven, the Trenton Six. Whether their insistance upon the rights of the Negro people is sincere or opportunistic may be determined by perusal of their press, which is full of admonitions to their own membership to rid themselves of racist concepts in their work and in their private lives. In similar fashion they have entered the lists on behalf of practically every national minority within the country, and in defense of the rights of those who are foreign born.

In foreign affairs they stand committed to peaceful coexistence between the two world systems of socialism and capitalism. They demand the abolition of colonialism and imperialism and the prohibition by all nations of atomic weapons. They propose negotiations as a solution to international tension, the expansion of east-west trade, and increased cultural exchange between all countries. They antedated Eisenhower by nine years in urging the American people to abandon the term "cold war."

They openly express keen interest in and sympathy with the aspirations of the peoples of the Soviet Union, which was the first country to embrace socialism. In this feeling they differ very little from republicans throughout the world who hailed the American Revolution of 1776 as the beginning of a new era in human affairs, and actively organized and propagandized against all attempts of kings and empires to throttle the infant state before it gained strength to defend itself.

All fourteen California defendants are vigorous advocates of socialism as the form of government best suited to the needs of the American people. Mrs. Oleta O'Connor Yates, California State Organizational Secretary of the Communist Party, herself a defendant, testified at great length in the trial concerning her understanding of Communist objectives.

She defined socialism as a system in which the means of production are owned by the whole people and produce for the whole people, rather than for the profit of an owning class. She testified that the change from capitalism to socialism is revolutionary in character; that the word revolution, indicating the fundamental nature of the change, carries no connotation of violence. She asserted the legal right of the American people to achieve such revolutionary change through democratic means. She stated her conviction that socialism can achieve power in the United States through the ballot box and without violence, and that so long as the democratic process remains unimpaired "there is no need for fearing strife or violence in the effecting of social change."

She declared that a revolutionary change to socialism in the United States is impossible "until the majority are convinced of its necessity";[1] that the majority are not presently so convinced; hence that socialism now or in the immediate future is not a demand of the Communist Party. Its purpose rather is to persuade people of "the ultimate need for socialism," and to lead them in achieving that revolutionary objective through peaceful means whenever they are convinced of its desirability or necessity. The constitution of the party enjoins its members to support and defend the Constitution of the United States and penalizes by expulsion those who advocate or employ violence. Until the majority of Americans support the objective of a socialist state, the Communist Party, while advocating socialism as the ultimate solution, struggle for the immediate needs and aspirations of the people within the framework of the present capitalist system.

However deeply one may disagree with the fore-

1. "When a great revolution finally breaks, it encounters virtually no internal opposition; it appears to unite the people rather than to separate them into hostile camps."—Encyclopaedia of the Social Sciences, Vol. XIII, page 371.

going summary of the defendants' sworn political beliefs, it cannot be said of these fourteen men and women that they have kept them secret, or have ever been reluctant to profess them to the widest possible number of persons.

THE JUDGE

William C. Mathes, presiding judge in the trial of the fourteen defendants, was appointed to the Southern District of California in 1945. He was in his fifty-third year and had served on the bench for six years when the trial opened. He was born in Texas and educated in the segregated schools of that state. He attended the University of Texas. While there he affiliated with a fraternity called Delta Tau Delta—a primitive distinction which joins him, by oaths too powerful ever to be revealed, in life-long brotherhood with the compiler of these notes. He received his law degree at Harvard. He is a member of the American Law Institute, the Masonic Lodge, the American Legion, and the University and Harvard Clubs.

The political dementia of the past decade has caused the American people to forget one of the soundest traditions of the founding fathers, which is that judges are not sacrosanct. They can, as Justice Holmes assures us, fall victim not only to private prejudice but to public pressure and transitory fears. Fanaticism can drive them, as it has driven former Supreme Court Justice Byrnes, to open subversion of the Constitution. Or, as Circuit Judge William Howard Taft's letters to his wife during the Pullman strike reveal, they can be impelled by partisanship to condone mass murder.

Indeed, if judges were as perfect as they are presently declared to be, we should not have been obliged to write into the criminal code so many laws to keep them honest. The number of them who have been caught and convicted for bribery, corruption, and general malfeasance is considerable enough to warrant all legislation calculated to encourage their virtue. Since they occupy positions of high public trust encompassing the power to punish their fellow citizens, they merit close watching at all times.

Readers of the trial record may sense in Judge Mathes' conduct evidence of prejudice sustained by barbaric rigidity of intellect. But those who sense it may themselves be prejudiced. One should therefore seek some objective factor in the case to throw light on the quality of the man who tried it.

In the course of the entire proceedings Judge Mathes was reversed by the Court of Appeals or by the Supreme Court eight times on the issue of reasonable bail for the defendants and three times on the issue of contempt, with two additional contempt appeals still to be decided. Error is to be expected as an occasional factor in the conduct of all affairs, and notable judges have been no exception. But repeated and consecutive error on the same issue does not represent occasional lapse. It can only arise from ignorance of the law, or contempt for it.

THE JURY

The men and women who sat in final judgment upon the fourteen prisoners represented, in many ways, an average American jury. They were predominantly middle-aged, middle-class, and often retired persons. But in one respect they were unique. They had been screened through a series of questions addressed by judge and prosecutor to determine their membership, or the membership of any of their relatives or friends, in a series of organizations running from the Communist Party itself to groups of the mildest liberal coloration. In this fashion it was made certain that the jury contained no person who had ever studied or been sympathetic to socialism.

On the face of it this appears reasonable enough. Certainly in a murder trial one would insist that persons who have studied or been sympathetic to murder be excluded from the jury. But this was not a murder trial, nor was it even a criminal trial in any ordinary sense. It was a political trial, involving political figures accused of a political crime. Since politics is determined by belief, it was therefore a trial involving what the defendants believed in. The jury was called upon to understand, interpret and pass judgment upon such beliefs. Viewed in this light, a process designed to screen from the jury all who might possess either knowledge of or sympathy with the beliefs at issue carries great significance.

A parallel might be found if Dr. Jonas Salk were to be tried on the charge that his vaccine infected certain persons instead of immunizing them as it was supposed to do; and if the judge and the prosecutor were to design a series of questions which resulted in the acceptance for jury duty of twelve persons who were ignorant of medicine and unsympathetic to its practice—a jury of naturopaths, let us say, or chiropractors, or faith-healers. Dr. Salk might well complain that the jury was not only incompetent to judge the medical issue in question, but was hostile to the science of medicine as well. Or, as has been written elsewhere, it is as if a jury of Moslems were called upon to determine the true doctrine of the Christian Eucharist.

The calculated selection—perhaps a necessary one from the government's point of view—of non-believers to pass upon the guilt of believers, as if belief itself could possibly be a crime under the Constitution, illustrates the legal and moral crisis inherent in the Smith Act itself and in all prosecutions flowing from it.

THE BOOKS

The formal charge against the defendants was that they had conspired to teach[2] and advocate the violent overthrow of the government of the United States. It was not charged that they *were* teaching and advocating such doctrine at the time of their arrest, but that they had conspired in the past to teach it at some unstated time in the future. They were to be punished not for what they had done but for what they might do.

Nor was it charged against these fourteen persons that they ever *had* advocated and taught the violent overthrow of the government. Had this been the charge, simple proof of written or spoken words of advocacy would have convicted them. But no such words existed. The government therefore resorted to the charge that they had in the past *conspired* to teach and advocate in the future.

In criminal conspiracy all persons associated together in the alleged conspiracy bear full and equal guilt for the illegal words or acts of every other individual in the group, and share equal punishments for his crime. If the group charged with conspiracy shares a common belief such as Marxism, and if the action they are charged with conspiring to achieve

2. "They teach, teach, teach . . . It's constant teaching, teaching, teaching."—U.S. Attorney Walter Binns in his summary to the jury.

is alleged to spring from the principles of Marxism, then any and all Marxist-Leninist writings may be used as evidence against them. Thus the charge of conspiracy made all of the defendants responsible not only for the individual words of each, but also for Marxist thoughts committed to paper twenty or fifty or a hundred years ago by men long dead, in historical circumstances which have ceased to exist.

Such, at least, was the theory of the government in prosecuting its case, and so it worked out in action as the trial developed. Thus it became a trial both of individuals and of philosophic principles. And because of this it inevitably degenerated into what Milton held to be the ugliest and most hateful of criminal prosecutions—a trial of books.

For a general definition of Marxism one should go to Marx and Lenin rather than to J. Edgar Hoover, just as in an earlier time it would have been wiser to seek a definition of the earth's motion from Galileo than from the seven cardinals of the Sacred Congregation of the Holy Office who forced him to recant.

"Marxism," says Lenin, "is the system of the views and teachings of Karl Marx." It is founded on philosophical and historical materialism; it employs the dialectical method which Marx defined as "the science of the general laws of motion both of the external world and of human thinking," and its political objective in socialism.

If this brief definition is unclear to the reader, it may be imagined how puzzling the exhaustive exploration into Marxism at the trial must have been to the jury. For Marxism deals with all aspects of the physical universe, including the ideas of man in every area of government, history, literature, science, and culture which his mind has discovered, created or investigated. Its theories and conclusions fill many hundreds of volumes, some of which have never been translated into English. It is, as the late Nobel Prize winning novelist Thomas Mann declared in 1948, a "doctrine which is, after all, the creation of great minds and great thinkers."

And so it was arranged that upon a jury composed of non-Marxists there fell the terrible burden of deciding which theory of two opposing theories about one aspect of a complex and interconnected system of thought called Marxism was the correct theory. If the jury failed to understand what the lawyers were talking about, or if it judged the issue wrongly, it can scarcely be blamed. Books and ideas and the people who read and think them ought not be charged with crime in the first place.

The government advanced the theory that violent revolution is an inherent principle of Marxism to which the defendants, as professed Marxists, were committed, supporting its contention with quotations from Marxist writings. The defense, stressing that government quotations referred to other countries existing in different historical circumstances, produced from the same Marxist writings other quotations affirming the possibility of peaceful transition from capitalism to socialism by legal means.

The sorry business of prosecuting people because of the books they read is best illustrated by specific examples of the prosecution's reasoning:

(1) There was a period in 1941 when, the United States then being at peace, the American Communist Party characterized the opening phases of World War II as an imperialist war. *The History of the Communist Party of the Soviet Union* reveals a period in 1917 when, Czarist Russia then being at war, Lenin urged the necessity of "converting the imperialist war into a civil war." Therefore the American Communist Party in 1941 conspired to convert World War II into a civil war, although it had never raised such a slogan or adopted such a program.

(2) During a period in Czarist Russia when trade unions were banned as illegal, Lenin wrote that members of the Communist Party should continue their trade union activity despite the ban; that they should engage in "illegal activities"—that is, activities in the prohibited trade unions designed to keep them functioning. Therefore American Communists, functioning in a country where trade unions have not been suppressed, are nonetheless similarly enjoined to engage in illegal activities.

The exaltation of such debauched logic to the status of "evidence," imputing to individuals personal and even criminal responsibility for admonitions written by men long dead to other persons in other nations in other times, offers an infallible method of tainting with evil motive even the most laudible act of citizenship, provided only that it is performed by one who has read and admired any of a wide variety of writings ranging from the Declaration of Independence to the works of Mark Twain.

But the prosecutor of the California fourteen went even further in his assault upon reason: either from arrogant certainty of conviction or out of contempt for the dignity of the jury, he neglected, insofar as most of the defendants were concerned, to establish that they had even read the carefully selected passages for which they were to be punished, much less that they had adopted the specific principles objected to for themselves and their work.

It is obvious that important and even fundamental conclusions cannot be reached by the recitation of mere excerpts torn from the context of a vast body of theoretical material. Federal Judge John M. Woolsey, in passing judgment on one volume instead of a thousand, had this to say about the matter:

> I have read *Ulysses* once in its entirety and I have read those passages of which the government particularly complains several times. . . . But there has been much written about it, and in order properly to approach the consideration of it, it is advisable to read a number of other books which have now become its satellites . . .

If books must be judged, that is the proper way to judge them. But if the books on trial with the fourteen California defendants had received similar careful and honest judgment the proceedings would have stretched over a decade, which is perhaps still another reason why systems of thought should not be brought to the dock as if they were crimes.

The first Republican President of the United States had firm ideas about forceful revolution. Speaking in the House of Representatives in 1848, he said: "Any people anywhere, being inclined and having the power, have the right to rise up and shake off the existing government and form a new one that suits them better." In his First Inaugural Address of 1861 he proclaimed to the nation: "This country, with its institutions, belongs to the people who inhabit it. Whenever they shall grow weary of the existing government, they can exercise their constitutional right of amending it, or their revolutionary right to dismember or overthrow it."

Because Dwight Eisenhower, like Abraham Lincoln before him, is a devoted Republican and the leader of his party, could any reasonable person or court or jury impute guilt to him for words spoken under entirely different circumstances by a man who died twenty-five years before Mr. Eisenhower was born? The government attorney in the California Smith Act trial would answer "Yes" to the query, for that is precisely how he won his conviction.

The Bible itself does not lack injunctions to kill, slaughter, ravish, burn, destroy, devastate, rebel, and overthrow. Some references are poetic and metaphorical. Others are specific and detailed. The book also contains extraordinarily beautiful invocations to charity and love and peace. Which set of commands are Christians to obey? And would it be possible to indict professing Christians for harboring those violent designs which are so deeply imbedded in the fabric of their theology?

The answer is that it would be possible if panic were generated, if the desire were present, and if men did not resist. It has in past times been possible and even laudable. Islamic tribunals had no difficulty in securing convictions upon precisely such a charge, while Christian magistrates punished Moslems for the same imputed crime. The difference between then and now is spelled out for Americans in the First Amendment to the Constitution.

The truth of the matter is that philosophies and systems of thought, like rivers and rocks and universes and men, change as new times confront them with new conditions. A great deal of what was true for science and history and economics and theology and politics in 1850 is untrue for them today. The rule is flat and without exception, whether applied to the concept of the physical properties of light or to the authority of the Pope in the definition of doctrine on faith and morals.

It would be a marvel indeed if Marxism had remained the only system inflexible to change, still binding its adherents to literal acceptance of every word and policy enunciated by its leaders a century or even a quarter-century ago. It would be even more marvelous in view of the fact that Marxism asserts that the physical universe, with everything in it including the ideas of man and the theory of Marxism itself, constitutes an inter-related and continuous process of change rather than a series of independent and static entities. Stalin made the point in this way: "Marxism does not recognize any immutable deductions and formulas, applicable to all epochs and periods."

The prosecution, contending contrariwise, bound the defendants to every word that had been written by their predecessors while denying the validity of every word they had written themselves. The dead became more real than the living, the past more vivid than the present. The government had found devils leaping from those Marxist books, and it sought to exorcise them by punishing living people.

Such is the process by which books are convicted in a legal trial. Actually it was not a trial at all. It was a ceremony; an act of legal mysticism performed before the altar of tribal gods in a time of fear.

THE WITNESSES

The government, in seeking to prove its charge against the fourteen defendants, brought forth two kinds of witnesses:

First: those who testified that they had hired themselves to the FBI for pay, and that the job they undertook was to penetrate the Communist Party and counsel with its leaders.

Second: those who were former members of the Communist Party and had broken with it or been expelled from it, and had thereafter placed themselves at the disposal of the FBI to reveal whatever confidences their former comrades had imposed in them.

Of the first group—paid police spies—no one will seriously question that they stood in relation to the FBI as employees stand in relation to a boss. A cook will prepare horsemeat or beef as the restaurateur requests; a carpenter will build a house as solid or flimsy as the contractor demands; a stenographer will type truth or fiction as his employer requires; and if any one of them fails to produce what is wanted, he will be discharged and his income will cease. The openly stated hostility of the FBI to the Communist Party justifies doubt that it would pay spies to secure information favorable to that organization. Indeed, it would not stretch credibility to suggest that the FBI requested damaging information about the Communist Party, and that any spy who failed to secure it would lose all value to his employer and quickly be separated from the payroll. The temptation to insure continued income by producing what is desired seems too obvious to belabor.

Of the second group—renegade-informers—it need only be recalled that the entire history of human culture as embodied in the works of its greatest philosophers, theologians, scientists, statesmen, and artists proclaims the informer an abomination. He who violates the trust of a friend ravishes the conscience of mankind. Once exposed, he has in all ages been shunned by honest men and his memory execrated.

Despite the high price of prosecution witnesses, their evidence was weak. The record contains naked examples, out of their own mouths, of perjury. The majority of them testified merely to the identity and affiliation of the defendants—identity and affiliation which the defendants had consistently asserted for themselves—and to their attendance at various meetings, without respect to what was discussed at such meetings. Against nine of the fourteen defendants there exists in the record not one assertion by any witness that they ever conspired to do anything.

Of the five remaining defendants, testimony connecting them with conspiracy to advocate violent overthrow was couched in words and phrases so vague that only interpretation by the witnesses of what the defendants really *meant* to say could imply any connection between them and a conspiracy. To illustrate: if I call upon citizens to rise and defend their liberties against the encroachments of the FBI, have I asked them to take up arms and overthrow the government, or have I urged them to assemble for political action in defense of their rights under the Constitution?

A final word on the prosecution witnesses: there exists a wide belief that they were merely dutiful citizens testifying about a crime they had witnessed. This is not entirely the truth. A man who has witnessed a murder and testifies concerning it in court is, indeed, a dutiful citizen. He does not expect thereafter to give testimony at other murder trials because he devoutly hopes never to witness another murder.

But many of the witnesses employed by the prosecution earn their living exclusively by testifying in political trials. If such trials stopped altogether, they would be out of work. They have no other occupation. Others who had not achieved a professional status nevertheless lived at government expense and were, in addition, paid substantial fees for their testimony. Their testimony was not, therefore, a disinterested act of citizenship; it was a commodity for which money had to be paid. The government wanted to buy testimony and the witnesses had it to sell and a deal was consummated between them.

Over strenuous objections by the prosecution, which viewed the whole matter as a morbid intrusion into areas too sensitive for public scrutiny, the government was obliged to reveal the precise sum it had paid to its covin of witnesses. The bill came to $48,303.52. The sum appears substantial, but when divided by fourteen it reveals how cheaply an American citizen can be deprived of his liberty.

THE VERDICT

The trial of the fourteen began on February 1, 1952. It would not end until August. For over six months the jurors listened to a debate on Marxist theories of violence and non-violence that must have perplexed them as greatly as a dissertation on the involvement of Euclidian space-time in Einstein's special theory of relativity in contrast to the *non*-Euclidian of his general theory.

While they sat each day in the courtroom and in their homes at night, the affairs of the world outside were not suspended. News of them, transmitted by radio, television, and the press, could not have escaped their notice. Five lawyers who had defended the first eleven Communists to be convicted under the Smith Act were sent to prison. American citizens were forbidden by the State Department to travel in the Soviet Union and countries friendly to it. Walter Winchell and his satellites filled the air with ominous tips from the FBI: predictions of war, rumors of imminent arrests, inside revelations of secret crises narrowly averted or yet to come.

Owen Lattimore was summoned before the Senate Internal Security subcommitte, then laying a basis for perjury charges against him which later, to the chagrin of the attorney general, were to be thrown out of court as invalid. Joseph M. Weinberg, the unfortunate "Scientist X" of newspaper espionage fiction, was indicted for perjury. That a Federal jury would acquit him of all charges could not then be surmised. Bernard M. Baruch, that venerable speculator whose merest grunt held oracular implications, created a sensation before the Senate Preparedness subcommittee by charging that the United States was losing the armament race. He issued a prophecy based on "warnings by the military" that the period through 1954 would be one of "the greatest danger to the United States." That 1954 would turn out to be the safest year since 1945 could not then be known.

Throughout the trial the Korean war continued its tragic course. Although its termination was dreaded in certain quarters,[3] the war was unpopular with the American people, and a trial of Communists was in progress, and the press was not hesitant in its daily coverage to connect the two. By June 23, the trial then being in its sixth month, the Air Force had lost over 1400 planes and had completed its 509,935th sortie over hostile territory. In the four months to follow it would fly 6500 sorties more to drop 42,000 tons of bombs and 200,000 gallons of napalm.

From February 18 to the end of the trial North Korean and Chinese prisoners rioted behind their barbed wire fences; and somehow every riot was laid by the press at the door of the defendants. There existed in the nation no community that did not cherish the memory of some young man, so very recently a boy, now dead or crippled in the conflict; and blame for this, too, was placed upon the prisoners in the dock. It was not a good time in which to stand

3. "Sudden peace would shake the United States' war-geared-economy."—*New York Herald-Tribune,* April 7, 1952.

"The possibility of a temporary truce haunts United States policy planners."—*Business Week,* April 12, 1952.

"The foreign policies of this country, Britain and France, have now entered a truly agonizing crisis. The cause is the so-called peace offensive now being carried on by the masters of the Kremlin."—*Washington Post,* April 16, 1952.

trial for a political belief that had been up-graded to treason.

In the final days of July the proceedings moved toward their denoument. By July 29, the last witness had stepped down from the stand. The last word of testimony had been placed in the record. Henceforth nothing could be added to it or deleted from it: the book was finally closed. The attorneys prepared for their appeals to the jury on the morrow. And it chanced on this particular day that a bolt of lightning issued from the nation's capital.

Senator Pat McCarran, chairman of the Senate Internal Security subcommittee, released to the press "with permission of FBI Director J. Edgar Hoover" what he described as a "long-secret report" in which, according to the Associated Press, the FBI claimed "documentary proof that the Communist Party in the United States '*teaches and advocates the overthrow of the United States government by force and violence.*'" Any thought of peaceful transition into socialism in the United States—a possibility the FBI had never previously admitted, but which the defendants contended was their objective—had been abandoned by William Z. Foster, in 1949, and the Communist Party thereafter stood committed to force and violence. Moreover, all reforms advocated by that party were mere deceits calculated to weaken and subvert the nation. (Beware of advocating peace, racial equality, higher wages, strong unions—they are Communist "deceits.")

Newspapers throughout the country gave the report no more than casual treatment. In Pasadena, six miles from the courtroom, it was worth exactly seven inches of type. But in Los Angeles, where the issue faced submission to a jury, the "long-secret report" took precedence over all else. It was broadcast hourly throughout the area, and for two days engaged the paramount attention of the Hearst and Chandler press. Timed with pin-point precision to the climax of the trial, proving the defendants' guilt in precisely the same words the government had used in its indictment, no man in whose breast patriotism still found shelter could believe them innocent.

That a "long-secret report" of such crucial significance immediately thereafter sank from sight and has never since been heard of as a serious matter. If the information it contained was true it should have engaged the world's attention for a decade. This being the case, why had the FBI kept it so long a secret? Why had its damning contents not been used in the first Smith Act trial in New York City? Why, indeed, had it not been submitted to the jury in the second trial at Los Angeles? And why has it not been used since?

If, on the other hand, it was a report whose contents at the time it was written had, like so many of its other triumphs, been secret only to the FBI; if, in fact, it was nothing but a compilation of excerpts from widely circulated and non-secret writings of Marx, Engels, Lenin, Stalin and William Z. Foster (which is what it was), then its providential appearance on that precise July 29 could be explained only by the fact that Mr. Hoover had been bedeviled with such a preposterous succession of bank robberies that he needed a major conviction to confirm his vigilance. If the people's money wasn't safe, at least their politics would be.

Judge Mathes denied a defense request for mistrial, admissable whenever anything happens in the course of a trial that might substantially affect the jury's verdict. He also denied a request that the jury be instructed to disregard whatever they may have read or heard of Mr. Hoover's dramatic revelation. He likewise denied a defense request that he question the jurors as to whether they had read or heard the report, and if so, if it had affected their verdict. The matter was sealed when the district court prohibited interrogation of any juror after the verdict on pain of contempt.

Two days later, at 4:25 on the afternoon of Thursday, July 31, the jury retired to consider a verdict. It was, taking all things into account, a rather remarkable group of men and women. Despite the fact that dissenting jurors in other trials involving real or alleged Communists had suffered publication of their names, anonymous threats and surveillance by the FBI; despite the clamor and vituperation, the alarms of war and threats of insurrection, there must have been doubt in their hearts.

Not until the following Tuesday did they arrive at a verdict of guilty.

THE SENTENCE

The prosecution and punishment of Communists can be made into a very good thing. U.S. District Judge Medina, who presided over the first Smith Act trial and innumerable banquet halls thereafter (in a recent speech he charged that the Communists during that trial maliciously encouraged his neurotic compulsion to jump out of windows), enjoyed promotion to the Court of Appeals. John F. X. McGohey, the U.S. attorney who prosecuted it, was rushed to the Federal bench. Two lesser prosecuting attorneys were elevated to the New York State Supreme Court and the United States District Court shortly after securing convictions in cases involving real or alleged Communists. Less glamorous figures have been elected to local office, embarked on careers in labor relations, or taken to the lecture circuit.

Despite the glitter of such rewards, there has been since the first Smith Act trial a tendency among federal jurists to sentence persons convicted under the Act to somewhat less than maximum terms in prison, with fines in proportion. But that passion for severity which consistently had driven Judge Mathes to violate the injunctions of the Eighth Amendment in relation to bail had not been cooled by his series of reversals. He imposed the maximum sentence—five years in prison and a fine of $10,000. It amounted, in more realistic terms, to 70 years of human life and $140,000 worth of human labor.

It has become an unfashionable cliche to point out that equal penalties for the rich and the poor are actually unequal, since the rich man's family eats while he is in jail and the poor man's family doesn't. We accept the inequality as a misfortune for which no relief can be devised. But we have always prided ourselves that under our form of government a man's property is sacred, and cannot be confiscated outright for any reason.

The proposition is only technically true. In practice the property of those who are not well-to-do is regularly confiscated through the device of fines. The combined assets of the fourteen defendants do not equal one-third of the fine assessed against them. Although the point made here relates to all convicted persons of modest means and not exclusively to political offenders, it is still worth making: the real sentence imposed by the court was five years imprisonment, five years of hardship for each family, and a confiscatory judgment outstanding, ready for instant execution if and when they acquire bank accounts or property of any consequence.

THE APPEAL

The defendants turned at once to the Court of Appeals, which responded on March 17, 1955 with a unanimous denial. Anticipating a commonplace rejection of the defendants' appeal, few were prepared for the curious distinction its three juridical authors would achieve by performing a passionate act of sanctification over the Alien and Sedition Laws of 1798—those repressive statutes which so enraged the Republic that civil war might have ensued had not an illegal resistance swept Jefferson to the presidency and caused them to lapse.

Referring to the Smith Act the three judges wrote:

That enactment, has been denounced as the first peacetime sedition law since 1798 [the Alien and Sedition Acts], although anyone who believes the country was not at war in 1940 [when the Smith Act was passed] does not squarely face the facts of life. If the founders were advised that statute [the Alien and Sedition Act] was necessary to meet the threat of the excesses of the French Jacobins then tending toward world-wide imperialism with a fatalistic zeal and a crusading flair and therefore compatible with the new Constitution, the act of 1940 [Smith Act] was probably advisedly deemed necessary to protect the national ideals and aspirations.[4]

Although denying review, the court hinted that the conviction of the fourteen defendants might involve

4. Material in brackets added by author for clarity.

something considerably beyond the scope of straight criminal law. "It may be" wrote the court, "that prospects of larger policy or changes in the look of international affairs should be viewed to fix the acts proved here in perspective. But, as we understand it, as a lower federal court that is not our function."

Clearly the court here viewed the jailing of Communists differently than the imprisonment of murderers or bank robbers. That "the acts proved here" (i.e., their guilt) might not be guilt in certain circumstances over which they had no control, must raise in disputatious minds a suspicion that the guilt or innocence of Communists depends on whether they criticize the government in a time of indecision and stress (when criticism is most essential to the democratic process), or in a time when affairs go so well that criticism is ineffectual or disregarded. If the suspicion has weight, it would appear that somewhere along the line the rights of citizens to due process have been rendered considerably more hazardous than the founding fathers intended.

THE SUPREME COURT

("clear and present danger")

The basic law governing all courts having jurisdiction over Communists under the Smith Act was laid down by the Supreme Court in 1951 when it affirmed the conviction of eleven national leaders of the Communist Party, in what has come to be known as the Dennis case. The defendants had been arrested on June 20, 1948; brought to trial in New York City before Judge Harold Medina on January 17, 1949; convicted on October 14 of the same year and sentenced to prison, along with their entire legal staff, on October 29. The Appellate Court sustained the convictions on August 1, 1950, in a decision written by Judge Learned Hand, and on June 4, 1951 the Supreme Court affirmed in a majority decision written by the late Chief Justice Vinson.

One need not entirely subscribe to the implication of Boswell's query whether Dr. Johnson "did not think that the practice of law, in some degree, hurt the nice feelings of honesty," in suggesting that the Court's affirmation of the Dennis conviction was not arrived at in its most shining hour. Nor would the Court itself desire that its action in that hour not be pondered and even questioned by citizens who may feel that somewhere in its decision their liberties suffered undue limitation.

The Supreme Court is an institution: its members are men. The very greatest justices have frequently revised or even negated their own previously written opinions. The collective entity which is the Court similarly has not hesitated to strike down previous rulings and replace them with new and opposite ones. While critics of the Court and litigants who have suffered from such dramatic reversals may attribute them to unconscious or even calculated error—and such must occasionally occur in all councils of men—a more reasonable explanation may be found in changed conditions not only within the Court but in those historical circumstances in which the Court functions.

The late Justice Jackson's observation that "We (the Court) are not final because we are infallible, but we are infallible only because we are final," is not entirely accurate. The finality of any decision of the Court—save its last on that unhappy day when it shall cease forever to exist—must be qualified by time. The Court's life cannot properly be viewed as a sequence of segmented finalities, but rather as a process functioning under the inflexible tyranny of one irrevocable rule: continuous change.

The Vinson Court in 1951 was a specific Court, differing in physical composition and historical time from the Stone Court which preceded it and the Warren Court that followed. In the Dennis appeal it encountered such a "great case" as perfectly to illustrate Justice Holmes' thesis that

> great cases like hard cases make bad law. For great cases are called great . . . because of some accident of immediate overwhelming interests which appeals to the feelings and distorts the judgment. These immediate interests exercise a kind of hydraulic pressure which makes what previously was clear seem doubtful, and before which even well-settled principles of law will bend.

Certainly there existed in 1951 "immediate overwhelming interest" which could appeal to the feelings and distort the judgment even of the wisest and most honorable of men. Probably not since the days of Taney and the Dred Scott case had the Court agreed to adjudicate a fundamental issue in circumstances so grave or so clamorous. Few would dispute that the Court's decision in the Dennis case, insofar as it touched upon the First Amendment, made "what previously was clear seem doubtful." Nor can it be denied that many persons antipathetic to the defendants' view nonetheless felt that affirmation had been made possible only by considerably bending "well-settled principles of law." If such, in fact, occurred, then the Dennis case met all of Holmes' qualifications for "bad law."

The Communist defendants arrived before the Supreme Court convicted of a conspiracy to *teach and advocate* violent overthrow of the government: they departed from it convicted of creating "a 'clear and present danger' of an *attempt to overthrow* the government by force and violence." The difficulty in reconciling the difference between the indictment and the Court's decision lies in the fact that it was not charged, and hence certainly not proved, that the defendants ever *did* teach and advocate.

How, then, to conclude that a conspiracy to speak certain words created the clear and present danger of an attempt at action described by them, although the words themselves had never been uttered?

The only possible solution lay in assuming what *would* have been advocated if words of advocacy had been spoken. Judge Medina had thoughtfully anticipated the need and provided the necessary assumptions under the guise of an instruction to the jury.

They could not, he told them, bring a verdict of guilty unless they found the defendants had

> conspired to organize a society, group and assembly of persons who teach and advocate the overthrow and destruction of the Government of the United States by force and violence and to advocate and teach the duty and necessity of overthrowing or destroying the Government of the United States by force and violence, with the intent that such teaching and advocacy be a rule or principle of action and by language reasonably and ordinarily calculated to *incite* such persons to action, all with the intent to cause the overthrow or destruction of the Government of the United States by force and violence *as speedily as circumstances would permit.*

Whether the jury could remember even for an hour that series of judicial statements which it confirmed as truth by the single word "guilty" is a matter for psychologists to decide. The reader may test himself by discovering if they remain with him that long, bearing in mind that we deal here with only one of many equally complex instructions which were read to the jury before it retired.

However curious the means by which it had been achieved, an assumption had been made, and it was on the record, and the gap between indictment and affirmation of sentence was therefore held to be filled.

Although judge and jury and Appellate Court and Supreme Court unanimously agreed that no words of advocacy had been spoken, still and all, the jury's verdict of guilty in combination with Judge Medina's inspired instructions, had proved "beyond a reasonable doubt" precisely what the words of advocacy *would* have been had they been spoken, what they would have been calculated to accomplish, and even the time at which the act they would have called for would occur. What reasonable defendant could ask for more?

With the exception of Justice Jackson the Court had agreed at the outset that the First Amendment's injunction against "abridging the freedom of speech, or of the press" was at issue, and that the Holmes test of "clear and present danger" must be applied. The lack of advocacy in the record had been squarely met by inferring what kind of speech would have been used had it been spoken. There remained only the final problem of determining whether the words that would have been spoken would have been dangerous enough to suppress.

The Court's majority opinion written by Chief Justice Vinson for himself and Justice Reed, Burton and Minton, quotes most of Holmes' famous test, which sets forth that

> the question in every case is whether the words used are used in such circumstances and are of such a nature as to create a clear and present danger that they will bring about the substantive evils that Congress has a right to prevent.

The majority opinion did not quote Holmes' next line which specified that limitations upon the First Amendment must be tested by the proximity (in time) and the degree (of danger) of the objectionable speech to the action that may flow from it. Certain speech is almost indistinguishable from action ("Ready, aim, fire!") and hence subject to restriction within the accepted meaning of the Amendment. Other speech is indeterminate ("Throw the rascals out!"), and may or not be punishable depending on whether it is uttered by an armed mob outside the White House or a politician on his rostrum. Still another kind of speech is so far removed in time from possible action ("The American people must ultimately overthrow capitalism and replace it with socialism") that the Court has always clothed it with immunity.

Since the Holmes opinion the Court on numerous occasions has emphasized the transcending importance of the First Amendment by further clarifying the Holmes test. The Court has held that there must be "grave and immediate danger." It has held that "the substantive evil must be extremely serious and the degrees of imminence extremely high before utterances can be punished." It has otherwise held that "the danger must not be remote or even probable; it must immediately imperil."

The Vinson opinion did not test the speech assumed in the Dennis case by such scrupulous standards. Instead it adopted for its own a new statement of the rule written by Judge Learned Hand of the

Appellate Court in sustaining the Dennis conviction. Judge Hand wrote that in each case involving a determination of the clear and present danger of action flowing from speech, the courts "must ask whether the gravity of the 'evil,' discounted by its improbability, justifies such invasion of free speech as is necessary to avoid the danger."

"Proximity" in the context of the Holmes rule can have no other definition than "nearness in time." The elimination of the proximity test from Judge Hand's rule permits the punishment of speech for actions which may flow from it not right now, not immediately, not even in proximate time—but in time itself, time undefined and unlimited, time which may extend into decades, or, indeed, may never arrive at all.

It may be conceded that discerning judges can accurately foresee those immediate and proximate evils which can be expected to flow from speech, and prohibit the speech to avoid the evil. But when jurists are called upon to punish speech because they think grave actions may probably flow from it "as speedily as circumstances will permit"—with no proof required that the circumstances will even occur during the lifetime of any person now living—the accepted order of things is reversed: clear and present means probable and remote, judgment down-grades itself to divination, and speech becomes more hazardous than action itself.

Justice Frankfurter had no illusions that the new concept of clear and present danger did not, in some degree, impinge upon the First Amendment. "The Smith Act and this conviction under it no doubt restrict the exercise of free speech and assembly," he wrote in one section of his opinion. And in another: "It is a sobering fact that in sustaining the conviction before us we can hardly escape restriction on the interchange of ideas." Although his view of limitations upon the power of the Court to protect freedom of speech impelled him to vote with the majority, the sombre eloquence of his opinion pays tribute to the gravity of the principles at issue.

Justice Douglas dissented flatly:

The freedom to speak is not absolute; the teachings of methods of terror and other seditious conduct should go beyond the pale along with obscenity and immorality. This case was argued as if those were the facts . . . But the fact is that no such evidence was introduced at the trial . . . The present case is not one of treason . . . We then start probing men's minds for motive and purpose; they become entangled in the law not for what they did *but for what they thought;* they get convicted not for what they said but for the purpose with which they said it. . . . I repeat that we deal here with speech alone, not with speech *plus* acts of sabotage or unlawful conduct. Not a single seditious act is charged in the indictment. To make lawful speech unlawful because two men conceive it is to raise the law of conspiracy to appalling proportions.

Justice Black, also dissenting, spoke similarly:

These petitioners were not charged with an attempt to overthrow the government. They were not charged with

> overt acts of any kind designed to overthrow the Government. They were not even charged with saying anything or writing anything designed to overthrow the Government . . . No matter how it is worded, this is a virulent form of prior censorship of speech and press, which I believe the First Amendment forbids. I would hold section three of the Smith Act authorizing this prior restraint unconstitutional on its face and as applied.

The two justices here were warning the Court against that fatal gap between indictment and affirmation which could be filled only by a proved act of advocacy. Perceiving that it had merely been stuffed up with the unspoken words of an assumption, they sought to prevent their colleagues from blessing a practice strikingly similar to that enunciated by Herman Goering: "People were arrested and taken into protective custody who had committed no crime but who, one might reasonably expect, would do all sorts of damage to the German state."

That such warnings proved futile is not remarkable, for the hour of decision found at least a few members of the Court in an extremely credulous state of mind. The Vinson majority, having excluded the actual trial record from its considerations, based itself upon certain broad conclusions which were drawn from that record by the Court of Appeals, among which it quoted as an established fact that "The Communist Party is . . . adept at . . . (the) use of . . . double-meaning language."

This judicial finding was derived from the Budenz

testimony, in which it was revealed to a startled jury that Communists use "AEsopian language"—i.e., the words they use do not mean what the dictionary says they mean. Thus anything they assert as truth must be taken as if accompanied by a leering wink. Such a novel and dynamic test for determining the credibility of witnesses, while not, perhaps, worthy of the unrestrained jubilation with which Judge Medina greeted it, should, at the very least, compel the admiration, if not the awe, of all the laity.

Testimony against a Communist, coming as it does from non-Communists or anti-Communists or former Communists, is single-meaning and true. But testimony from a Communist in his own behalf is double-meaning, hence a ridiculous falsehood. Application of the test cuts down work and immediately simplifies the trial record, since all double-meaning defense evidence is automatically negated. This leaves nothing but single-meaning, which is what everybody but the defendant was striving for in the first place. The score at the end of the trial as to credibility of witnesses cannot fail to stand at 100 percent for the prosecution to a well-deserved zero for all those mischievous avowals of innocence.

Lest the charge of exaggeration be made, the record of the second New York trial reveals the United States attorney pressing his already handsome advantage even further. Embarrassed by the government's paucity of evidence, he used what he lacked to convince the jury how much he really had. The defendants, he contended, being skilled conspirators, had hidden the precise evidence which he needed to damn them. It's very absence proved how cunning they were, and how dangerous, and therefore how guilty.

No one smiled. Nor did anyone smile at the Supreme Court's majority finding that there existed on the day of the defendants' arrest in June 1948, a clear and present danger that they would attempt to overthrow the government by force and violence.

Justice Douglas's perplexity on this point was considerable:

> Communism has been so thoroughly exposed in this country that it has been crippled as a political force . . . How it can be said that there is a clear and present danger that this advocacy will succeed is, therefore, a mystery . . . It is safe to say . . . that the invisible army of petitioners is the best known, the most beset, and the least thriving of any fifth column in history. Only those held by fear and panic could think otherwise.

There had been no attempt at revolution thirteen years earlier when the Communists were said to number over 100,000 members whose doctrine might well have appealed to 14 million unemployed men and women. Since then J. Edgar's annual reports had charted a steady drop in membership: 60,000 by 1947; 42,000 by 1952; some 22,000 today.

Upon Republican charges that the land fairly teemed with Communists, President Truman regularly poured the scorn of one who knew the truth.

Not once in the course of his two administrations did the President warn the country that there was even a remote—much less a clear and present—danger of an attempted Communist revolution. He was of the opposite opinion. "We know that the greatest threat to us does not come from the Communists in this country," he declared after the Dennis trial and before the Supreme Court affirmed the conviction. He added that ". . . they have steadily been losing ground since their peak in 1932 . . ." Clearly the President differed with the Court as to the internal stability of the Republic and the imminent danger of revolution.

Revolutions there had been in considerable numbers, and most of them in that hemisphere of which the United States avowed itself the economic and moral leader. Since the end of World War II the governments of Argentina, Bolivia, Cuba, Costa Rica, Peru, Venezuela, El Salvador, Guatemala, Colombia, Paraguay and Nicaragua had been overthrown by force and violence. But no one in the United States, not even Senator McCarthy, had ever attributed this appalling sequence to Communists. They were revolutions of the right, and the new governments they lifted to power received instant blessing from the State Department.

The most powerful government in the world, trembling before the threatened assault of eleven Communist Party officials and their followers, might have sought reassurance by turning its eyes toward a more stable area, where the Communist Parties in

France and Italy have regularly polled millions of votes. In the United States the Communist Party, with one member for every 3200 inhabitants, couldn't even get on the ballot; but every fourth Frenchman voted Communist, and every fourth Italian, and they had been doing it steadily since the end of the war. The United States was prosperous beyond all dreaming; France and Italy were prostrated by continuous tremors of economic collapse and internal dissension. Only a hundred and fifty miles from their frontiers stood the Red Army, larger than any land force in the world.

Yet in the midst of those precise circumstances which the State Department warns are most auspicious for violent revolution, there had been no revolution. There had been no danger of revolution. The only conceivable danger had been that the Communists might achieve power through free and democratic choice of the majority at the ballot box—which the State Department has always proclaimed the final test of legitimacy. Beyond this there had been teaching and advocacy of Marxism. There had been organization and propaganda and voting. There had been no attempt at revolution.

Neither would there be in the United States. Nor did there live during the three years of the Dennis case a single Government official who believed or feared there would be. Nor did the people believe it either.

The tragic dilemma which brought the Court to its

destination in 1951 cannot be explained in law or reason because it bore no relation to either. The thing that happened was properly not a trial at all; it was an event. Such events differ from ordinary trials in that they must be carried forward by political rather than legal means, and must serve political rather than legal ends.

The event does not occur because a policeman stumbled across a revolution. A decision in America to outlaw a political party involves grave consequences which must be evaluated at the very highest levels of government. Political suppression in a parliamentary democracy functioning under a written constitution reverses the legal process which the nation has set up as a measuring stick for the world to judge it by. It serves as an international storm signal, informing the world of impending domestic convulsion or foreign adventure.

The pattern is no stranger to the foreign offices of the world. Napoleon tried it, and Napoleon the Lesser, and Metternich, and Mussolini, and Hitler. Since no government on earth believes there exists any danger of an attempt to overthrow the United States by force and violence, internal revolution is immediately ruled out of diplomatic consideration, and the attention of the powers is directed toward that foreign objective which motivates the policy of internal suppression. The ugly issue of war, or a plan for war, obtrudes itself upon the international scene.

Once the event has begun, the whole prestige of the

government is at stake. The trial judge well knows the significance of the event, and how it differs from an ordinary criminal trial. The intermediate court is itself an integral part of the government whose honor is at issue. As the conflict moves into the chambers of the Supreme Court, the event approaches its climax. Ardently though both appellant and Court may desire to defer judgment to calmer times when passion and politics and power have surrendered their claims, it cannot be deferred.

Both sides have been swept by history toward a rendezvous that neither chose nor desired nor can avoid. Individual wills now count for nothing against the larger forces in movement. The defendants appeal to the Court because they cannot do otherwise; the Court consents to adjudicate because it dares not refuse; the decision finally extorted by history reflects the Court's evaluation not of law but of necessity.

THE SUPREME COURT

("the inflammable nature of world conditions")

The dazzling illumination cast upon the physical universe by Einstein's work could not have been possible without the equivalent, at least, of the

Lorentz transformations, which enabled science to comprehend the universe as a universe of events rather than the old universe of points, and led to the conclusion that "every event is characterized by the place and time of its occurrence."

If we similarly view the Supreme Court's extraordinary decision in the Dennis case as an event, an examination of the time at which it occurred should illuminate the real fear—which could not possibly have been of an attempt at revolution—that impelled the Court to proclaim an absurdity.

It was a time of war, real or incipient. It was a time when the mildest admonition to foreign governments was clothed with language that half a century before would have brought instant declarations of war; a time when admirals and generals amused themselves in public by boasting of an absolute supremacy which made possible the destruction of nations or groups of nations; a time when statesmen on the highest level conducted debates—most of them, unfortunately, in public—on the desirability of making war to avoid war, and proceeded instantly to bewitched considerations of when it would be best for us to do it; a time when the sullen star of McCarthy, rising above the jungle horizon and glowing ever more brightly as it approached its zenith, stirred old and ugly passions to the celebration of rituals now apprehended with disgust. Mere invocation of the period demonstrates how very long ago it was, not in years, but in the changed national consciousness.

The merits of the cold war are not here at issue; absolute virtue resided with neither side and errors, many of them already admitted, were made by both. The cold war was a fact, and it was the cold war rather than the fear of any domestic disorder which became the paramount fact in the Court's consideration of the Dennis case.

The Vinson opinion recognized the fact in the following words:

> The formation by petitioners of such a highly organized conspiracy, with rigidly disciplined members subject to call when the leaders, these petitioners, felt that the time had come for action, coupled with the inflammable nature of world conditions, similar uprisings in other countries, and the touch-and-go nature of our relations with countries with whom petitioners were in the very least ideologically attuned, convince us that their convictions were justified on this score.

Frankfurter's concurring opinion similarly referred to "the setting of events in this case," and quoted George F. Kennan, a state department expert then more famous than now, to the effect that "The American Communist Party is today, by and large, an external danger." Justice Frankfurter took judicial notice "that the Communist doctrines which these defendants have conspired to advocate are in the ascendancy in powerful nations who cannot be acquitted of unfriendliness to the institutions of this country."

Frankfurter's reference to the Soviet Union as a nation that "cannot be acquitted of unfriendliness" is an exquisite, though unconscious, reflection of the concept of relations between powers which then prevailed in the government. Unfriendliness to us had become a crime for which the culprit sovereign power, if only it recognized our moral authority, ought to stand trial in our courts and receive therefrom conviction or acquittal. It was this odd consciousness of absolute right which, causing men to believe we could "lose" a China we never owned,[5] impelled them to the dangerous idea that we could gain (through war) a Russia we never lost.

That foreign rather than domestic fears governed the majority was also clear to Justice Douglas, who declared, "We might as well say that the speech of petitioners is outlawed because Soviet Russia and her Red Army are a threat to world peace." But even using this as an excuse, which the majority plainly did, Douglas will have none of it. He insists that "It is safe to say that the followers of the creed of Soviet Communism are known to F.B.I.; that in case of war with Russia they will be picked up overnight as were all prospective saboteurs at the commencement of World War II . . ." Douglas understands perfectly that the expressed fear of an attempt at revolution is nonsense-language for larger fears based upon expectations of war. And he declares the danger not great enough to punish men for what it is assumed they may then do.

Justice Holmes, whose ideas have so powerfully

5. Twenty-two years later: "The truth is that China was no one's to 'lose' except China's."—Harrison E. Salisbury, New York Times Service, October 11, 1971.

affected the Court's thinking through recent decades, once said: "The primary rights and duties with which jurisprudence busies itself again and again are nothing but prophecies . . ." His use of the word prophecies rather than predictions is interesting.

A prediction can be verified; a prophecy has to be fulfilled. A judge may accurately predict those clear and present and immediate dangers which will flow from current speech; but he can only prophesy those which he thinks will flow from it at some unspecified point in remoter time. The idea of judges as prophets has plagued the courts ever since Holmes wrote of it, and they are naturally eager to avoid decisions which might involve prophecy. Justice Frankfurter's opinion frankly states the dangers:

To make validity of legislation depend on judicial reading of events still in the womb of time—a forecast, that is, of the outcome of forces at best appreciated only with knowledge of the topmost secrets of nations—is to charge the judiciary with duties beyond its equipment . . . It is as absurd to be confident that we can measure the present clash of forces and their outcome as to ask us to read history still enveloped in clouds of controversy.

Justice Jackson, who avoided all by confirming on a simple point of criminal law, pointed out to the Court that they and he had affirmed for quite different legal reasons, and that the basis of his colleagues' affirmation was impossible to defend, since:

If we must decide that this Act and its application are constitutional only if we are convinced that petitioner's conduct creates a "clear and present danger" of violent overthrow, we must appraise imponderables, including international and national phenomena which baffle the best informed foreign offices and our most experienced politicians. We would have to foresee and predict the effectiveness of Communist propaganda, opportunities for infiltration, whether, and when, a time will come that they consider propitious for action, and whether and how fast our existing government will deteriorate . . . No doctrine can be sound whose application requires us to make a prophecy of that sort in the guise of a legal decision. The judicial process simply is not adequate to a trial of such far-flung issues. The answers given would reflect our own political predelictions and nothing more.

We have hitherto noted that the Dennis case and all that flowed from it had no basis in law and could not possibly culminate in a legal decision. The case sprang from the worldwide contention of forces whose enormity could not be comprehended, from the specific political circumstances of its period, and the Court's decision, wrested from it in a time of crisis, had also to be political. Justice Jackson in the foregoing passage probed straight to the heart of the Court's dilemma. Its affirmation of the Dennis conviction could not possibly be other than "*prophecy . . . in the guise of a legal decision.*"

The Court did not fear and was not talking about the danger of "an attempt to overthrow the Government by force and violence." What it did most gravely fear was the danger of an attempt by one side or the other to declare war. An historic crisis had compelled the Court to look into the future. It looked, and it prophesied war.

Five years later, in 1956, the clear and present danger of an attempted revolution which the Court proclaimed in 1951 to have existed since 1948 had not manifested itself in action of any kind. A stable government presides unchallenged over a tranquil people. The prophesied war did not occur and does not presently even threaten. The issue is not war but peace, and diplomacy by threat has, on both sides, given way to diplomacy by negotiation.

History having reversed the Court's prophecy, it became inevitable that the Court itself would undertake to review once more the conflicting claims of the Smith Act and the First Amendment.

CERTIORARI

The government, in the Dennis case, declared before the Court of Appeals that "These appellants are the organizers and leaders of the Communist Party and they, above all other persons in the United States, threaten serious injury to the national interests protected by the Smith Act." Similarly, both the Appellate and the Supreme Courts had emphasized that Dennis and his fellow defendants were "the leaders, these appellants."

It might be presumed that once these dangerous

men who comprised the national leadership of the Communist Party were safely in prison the clear and present danger of an attempted revolution would somewhat subside. But the reverse occurred; the danger of revolution appeared to increase in direct ratio to the number of Communist leaders jailed. Since that first case, Smith Act trials or indictments have been carried through in New York, California, Maryland, Pennsylvania, Michigan, Missouri, Washington, Colorado, Ohio, Connecticut, Hawaii, and Puerto Rico.

Indeed, the Attorney General no longer pretends to limit his prosecution to national leaders. State and county and even city and group leaders, as well as individuals charged with mere membership, are now brought to dock in increasing numbers for a crime which the distinguished British lawyer, Mr. D. N. Pritt, has somewhat wonderingly described as "mere advocacy of the most widely held political doctrine in the world."

Government attorneys and federal judges in all the Smith Act cases have offered the most elaborate reassurances to the jury, and hence to the press and the people, that Smith Act prosecutions do not represent an attempt to suppress the Communist Party itself; that membership in the Communist Party is not considered by them a criminal act; that the party leaders on trial were not indicted because they were Communists—a legal thing to be—but because, as Communist leaders, they had conspired to divert the party to certain ends that were not legal.

Having thus in principle rendered unto the people

the things which are the people's, the Department of Justice proceeded to render unto Caesar not only Caesar's portion, but the people's as well. It set about to do what it had declared it was not going to do, namely, to indict and try individuals on the simple charge of Communist membership. Such persons were not charged with conspiring to do anything. They were charged, for the first time in American history, with belonging to a legal political party. Dr. Albert Blumberg's indictment, for example, simply declared that "the defendant has been a member of the said Communist Party."

Under this curious version of free political choice in a multiparty democracy, eight men have been indicted under that section of the Smith Act which punishes anyone who has become "a member of, or affiliated with, any such society, group or assembly of persons, knowing the purposes thereof." Claude Lightfoot of Chicago, Junius Scales of North Carolina, John Noto of Buffalo, and Dr. Albert Blumberg of Baltimore have been tried, convicted and sentenced to five years in prison. Max Weiss of Illinois, Michael Russo of Massachusetts, Emanuel Blum of Indiana and John Hellman of Montana presently await trial.

It is worthy of note that under the wording of the Act former Communists may be indicted as well as present ones, and that the word "affiliate" has in the past been so broadly interpreted by the government as to include persons who have never been members of the Communist Party but may have worked politically with Communists, or even persons who advocate action on specific issues which Communists also advocate.

As the convictions mounted in number and kind, the lower judiciary proved once more that a grant of power for partial suppression must inevitably reach out for total suppression. The Court's decision in the Dennis case, encroaching as it did upon the First Amendment, still set forth certain legal standards by which Smith Act trials had to be conducted in the future. But the forces set in motion by the Dennis decision, the stress of exterior political circumstances, and the federal policy of reward-for-conviction, have in subsequent trials lured presiding judges and U.S. district attorneys into shortcuts calculated to bypass most of the impediments interposed by the Dennis decision between future Smith Act defendants and the penitentiary.

The rule of the Dennis case requires the judge to instruct the jury that it may convict only if it finds that the teaching and advocacy of the defendants employed "language reasonably and ordinarily calculated to incite persons to such action" as might be called for. Both prosecution and defense requested Judge Mathes in the California case similarly to instruct the jury. The judge refused, and the government, revising its position, now contends the instruction wasn't important anyhow. "At the very least," wrote Justice Rutledge in another case, "the line must be drawn between advocacy and incitement." If Judge Mathes has his way, incitement to violent action no longer need be proved against a citizen's speech; he may be imprisoned for teaching of ideas alone.

In the Dennis case it was held necessary to find that the defendants, *acting jointly as a group,* reconstituted the Communist Party in 1945 and controlled it as an instrumentality for the purpose of advocating the overthrow of the government. Judge Mathes did not require proof of joint action as a group against the California defendants, and evidence of joint action among all of them is completely lacking. Such joint action (for peace, against racial discrimination, etc.) as is proved among a few of them nowhere involves activity charged in the indictment. This second encroachment upon the Dennis decision asserts that all Communists, or at least all office-holders in the Communist Party, may be found guilty of criminal conspiracy without regard to what they have said or done.

The law at the time of the Dennis trial did not require proof of an overt act forwarding the conspiracy charged. It has since been amended, making it incumbent upon the prosecution in the California trial to prove such overt acts. The prosecution met this requirement by placing the defendants at two perfectly legal public meetings attended by hundreds of people. Under the Constitution, under the decisions of the Supreme Court, and as a matter of law, attendance at a lawful public meeting cannot be turned into an overt act in the advancement of a criminal conspiracy. Judge Mathes and the Court of Appeals dissent.

On the matter of "clear and present danger" which lay at the heart of the Dennis case, Judges Mathes' abnormal propensity to error gained ascendancy once more. Judge Medina, basing himself upon the Dennis evidence, ruled as a matter of law that if the defendants were guilty as charged, their acts created a clear and present danger of an attempt at revolution. The higher Courts agreed, and held the First Amendment rule of clear and present danger to be the central Constitutional question at issue in the case.

But when requested to rule upon the issue of clear and present danger, or to submit it to the jury, Judge Mathes once more declined. The question of clear and present danger, he explained, had no bearing on the case. The conspiracy charged against the defendants was criminal, the speech used was criminal, and the question of whether it created a clear and present danger made no difference at all.

It seems clear that unless a person has the power to bring about the evil, there obviously can be no danger of him doing so; hence that his power to bring about the evil must be proved before it can be established that there is clear and present danger of the evil occurring. In ruling that clear and present danger had no bearing on the case, Judge Mathes automatically eliminated from the trial any consideration of whether the state and county officials on trial actually had it in their power to bring about the national revolution they were alleged to desire.

He held that they could be convicted regardless of whether there was in the remote future any possibility of danger arising from their speech, and, indeed, even if no danger should ever arise from it, since the speech itself constituted the crime. He not only refused to submit the question of their power to bring about the danger to the jury, but himself declined to take judicial notice that no evidence relating to such power existed in the record.

The Supreme Court in the Dennis case, after ruling that "clear and present danger" was paramount, went on to declare that in the future "where there is doubt as to the intent of the defendants, the nature of their activities, or *their power to bring about the evil,* this Court will review with the scrupulous care demanded by our Constitution."

On October 17, 1955, the Supreme Court, Chief Justice Warren presiding, granted certiorari to the fourteen California defendants. It was not such limited certiorari as the Vinson Court had granted the Dennis defendants, wherein the trial record was excluded: it was full certiorari, including the trial record itself and everything connected with it, as well as all constitutional issues involved. On December 12, 1955, the Court similarly granted certiorari to the Pennsylvania defendants.

The Court had fulfilled its promise.

THE PEOPLE MUST REVIEW

Proscription as policy in a parliamentary democracy contains within itself three fatal errors:

(1) It disgraces the nation before the world, breeds contempt for its envoys, hatred for its citizens, and disaster for its foreign policy.

(2) If successful, its triumph is never celebrated over the principles of the proscribed, but over the ruins of the government it set out to protect and was, in the end, obliged to destroy.

(3) It almost never succeeds, and such success as it may enjoy is always transitory.

There presently exists in the world no government or institution or system of thought that in earlier time has not been proscribed and its adherents branded criminals. The record might even be interpreted as proof positive that proscription offers the surest guarantee to the proscribed not only of survival but of triumph.

Governments and ambitious men within governments cannot be warned too solemnly that there are certain things men will not do; certain commands they will not obey; certain intrusions they will not tolerate; certain thoughts they will persist in thinking. Not mercy but wisdom commands the government to speak softly and tread lightly along those perilous avenues which approach the conscience of the individual citizen. They lead to sacred territories whose invasion in the name of the national interest may be repelled by the invocation of a loftier principle which exalts patriotism above mere obedience.

The late Chief Justice Charles Evans Hughes wrote in the MacIntosh case,

> In the forum of conscience, duty to a power higher than the state has always been maintained. The reservation of that supreme obligation, as a matter of principle, would unquestionably be made by many of our conscientious and law-abiding citizens.

The most extraordinary aspect of the decade which extended from 1945 to 1955 is the stubborn refusal of the people to surrender their democratic heritage, to accept the inevitability of world-wide war and all the losses it would involve. The policies of the Government during that appalling time were not the policies of the people. Had they been we should long since have become involved in war. The hysteria was not national. It was the private fear of a comparatively small group who conspired to carry through policies that were abhorrent to the majority.

True, the people were silenced as the hateful shadow of the FBI advanced from the corner streetlight into the yard, and from the front porch finally into the house itself, into every room and closet, even falling upon books that lay unguarded by the fire. The people were sickened by the swarm of voyeurs who had crept into the national residence with letter-openers and tiny cameras and the most delicate microphones to spy and make notes upon matters that mankind even in the time of the swamp and the forest and the cave had felt to be sacred.

They were silenced and sickened, but they were not intimidated beyond the degree of natural prudence, and they resolutely refused to be stampeded. The self-tormented mobs of the Know-Nothing era did not move through the streets. The eager vigilante groups of World War I did not reassemble. The anticipated stampede toward Fascism did not occur.

Thousands of men and women found their careers in ruins; hundreds were delivered into jail; and two, at least, were probably murdered: but the fact remains that a national campaign of unparalleled ferocity, enduring a full decade, sustained by the total commitment of press, radio and cinema, limited not at all by truth or even decency, failed to convince the people.

Its failure is measured at the summit by the Geneva Conference and the broad vistas of peace which can be found beyond it, and at the level of commonplace life by a swift-moving sequence of small events which will be perceptible only as their inevitable effect upon the larger design is made manifest. It is quite impossible to exaggerate the glories of good sense.

This heartening new atmosphere, in which even the face of a stranger on the bus seems somehow brighter because of a pervasive feeling that it will be seen again as the face of a human being rather than a stain of liquefied matter on the periphery of an atomic explosion, has impelled men to take new stands and give expression to long-held faith. The most distinguished persons in the country now enter the arena, clamoring before the Hennings Committee for an end to inquisition, boldly petitioning the Government and the Court for revocation of the McCarran Act, speaking in churches and schools and assemblies for an end to domestic repression and foreign adventure.

Shortly before Christmas Day in 1955, a group of 42 distinguished Americans led by Mrs. Franklin D. Roosevelt, Henry Steele Commager, Lewis Mumford, Elmer Rice and Norman Thomas gave practical example to the nation by addressing a public appeal to President Eisenhower. They wrote:

> We respectfully urge you, to grant an amnesty commuting the sentence of the 16 men and women now in prison under the Smith Act (Alien Registration Act of 1940) to time already served, and to use your influence to secure the postponement of trials in the 180 cases presently awaiting trial court or appeals court decisions under the act.

Asserting their fundamental disagreement with the philosophy of the Communist Party, and referring to Justice Black's magnificent dissent in the Dennis case, they continued: "The indictments and convictions in these cases were carried through in a period of the 'cold war' and in an atmosphere often marked by hysteria." Amnesty and postponement, they declared, would "give proof of our confidence in democratic institutions" and "contribute toward peace in the world about which you are so deeply concerned . . ."

Judge Learned Hand once wrote: "I wonder if we do not rest our hopes too much upon constitutions, upon laws and upon courts . . . . Liberty lies in the hearts of men and women; when it dies there, no constitutions, no law, no court can save it . . ." Mrs. Roosevelt and her colleagues, while noting that the Court has agreed to review the Smith Act, give answer in their public appeal to Judge Hand's doubts. They are not content to rest their hopes exclusively upon the Court. They stand with the great German jurist, Rudolph von Jhering, in concluding that "the life of the law is a struggle," and they have openly, energetically, and honorably entered the struggle.

As the Supreme Court moves to review the Smith Act convictions, the American people must also review them and enter the struggle to overthrow them. The old and not very valorous strategy of tossing Communists to the wolves in despairing hope that the civil rights of all others will then be spared has not worked. The appetite of the Department of Justice and the FBI has proved insatiable.

Because the Smith Act was allowed to supersede the Constitution, the conclusions flowing from it have made 14 million of the nation's total working force of 64 million the subjects of confidential files; 5 million members of the armed forces have been subjected to loyalty investigation: 3 million defense workers have been processed; half a million workers in the Atomic

Energy Commission have been checked, and another half million seamen and port workers have been placed by Congress under security clearings.[5] A shotgun designed to kill Communists is not selective when fired into any area of national life. It has, on occasion, even winged a Republican.

The Smith Act is the keystone of the whole structure of suppression; its collapse will undermine all other parts of a hateful edifice. Men once more will be able to move freely on the earth to which they were born. They will be able to work as they wish at any vocation they choose without enduring the ignominy of test oaths imposed to make them shiver before the face of authority. They will be able to subscribe to such domestic or foreign magazines as they want; to write to their friends in joyous certainty the message will not be violated by the suspicious eye of Federal police; they will be able to associate as proud and free-born citizens with whomever they please, and to speak at their work and sleep in their beds without experiencing, now and then, that curious and shameful little spasm of trepidation that asks: am I heard, am I watched, is there a microphone about?

The essence of all the Smith Act trials was summarized by Justice Black in his solemn dissent to the Dennis conviction:

> Public opinion being what it now is, few will protest the conviction of these Communist petitioners. There is hope, however, that in calmer times, when present pres-

5. *Reader's Digest,* November 1955, page. 138.

sures, passions and fears subside, this or some later Court will restore the First Amendment liberties to the high preferred place where they belong in a free society.

The free society to which Justice Black has dedicated a distinguished career cannot be sustained by passive hope. It requires sturdier support against its enemies. Men who love a free society must fight for it. Larger interests than their own are involved: the liberty it engenders belongs to their children and their children's children, and ought not be cheaply surrendered by the fathers.

A nation may be betrayed from within and survive; it may be betrayed from without and survive; but nature and history forbid it to betray itself.

Afternote

Convictions of the fourteen California Smith Act defendants were reversed by the United States Supreme Court on June 17, 1957. The majority opinion, written by Justice John Marshall Harlan, dismissed all charges against five defendants, and prescribed rules of evidence and Constitutional standards for retrial of the remaining nine. On motion of the United States District Attorney, after six months of trial and almost six years of litigation, all charges were dismissed and the case was dropped.

Honor Bright and All That Jazz

IN THE AUTUMN OF 1947, nineteen members of the Hollywood film community were summoned to Washington for political purification before the House Committee on Un-American Activities. They were not the first celebrants of the committee's bizarre ritual, but their motion-picture background made them temporarily the most famous, or—depending on how fastidious you are and what you paid for your seat—the most notorious.

There ensued a week of clamors and alarms the like of which the Republic hadn't known since J. P. Morgan tried to explain why he wanted to marry a midget. He never did get it straight, and neither did the chaps from Hollywood. After the first eleven of them flunked its version of the Apostles' Creed, the committee abruptly dismissed the eight witnesses who remained, and adjourned in dudgeon.

The eleventh witness was Berthold Brecht, who received so strong an impression of the committee's non-benevolence that he grabbed the first Swissbound plane out of LaGuardia and never again set foot on free American soil. He seemed to have the uncomfortable feeling, based, perhaps, on earlier hassles over un-German activities, that all those doctors of humane letters who earned their bread by writing about his plays and describing his genius would forget, somehow, to set the alarm clock on the day he went to jail. The more one thinks on it the more plausible the idea seems.

Those he left behind had no taste for martyrdom and no conception of the storm their conduct would arouse. To this day I suspect there is not one of them who feels anything but pleasure when he opens the morning paper and finds his name not there. They did not ask to play the parts assigned them by the committee, and, like any other group of even passably intelligent men, would have ducked the game altogether had the chance arisen. They were as confused as anybody else, and probably made more mistakes. They were, after all, down there on a ballfield which is error's favorite breeding ground, while Brer Rabbit sat cool in the bleachers and judged form.

What actually happened to them was almost as simple as changing pig to pork, although it took longer. Charged with trying to subvert Hollywood to communism by a gaggle of witnesses friendly to the committee, including George Murphy, then a leading man, now the junior Senator from California, and another leading man named Ronald Reagan, who may be California's next governor and Goldwater's candidate for the Presidency, the Ten took the stand in October, 1947, invoked the First Amendment, and declined to reveal whether they were, or ever had been, members of the Communist Party and the Screen Writers' Guild. In November they were cited for contempt of Congress, a misdemeanor. In December they were blacklisted by the producers in a public statement known as the Waldorf Agreement. The following year saw them indicted, arraigned, tried, convicted, sentenced, and released on bail pending appeal.

During the first phase of the battle their principal support came from the film community itself. Those actors, actresses, directors, producers, writers, musicians, and artists who formed the Committee for the First Amendment took to the air in a series of remarkable broadacsts, and addressed a petition to the House for relief from "the abuse of civil liberties we believe to have occurred at those hearings."

A few weeks later, Representative John E. Rankin, whose parliamentary legerdemain had made the Committee on Un-American Activities a permanent committee of the House rather than a temporary one, and who was himself its senior Democratic member, rose in the House to attack those who dared to criticize its conduct. It is impossible to understand the spirit of the times, the quality of the committee, or the issues confronting the Ten, outside the context of what he said, and what no member of the Committee—not even Representative Richard M. Nixon—disavowed or sought in any way to ameliorate:

They sent this petition to Congress, and I want to read you some of these names. One of the names is June Havoc. We found out . . . that her real name is June Hovick. Another one was Danny Kaye, and we found out his real name was David Daniel Kamirsky. Another one here is John Beal, whose real name is J. Alexander Bliedung. Another is Cy Bartlett whose real name is Sacha Baraniev. Another one is Eddie Cantor, whose real name is Edward Iskowitz. There is one who calls himself Edward Robinson. His real name Emanuel Goldenberg. There is another one here who calls himself Melvyn Douglas, whose real name is Melvyn Hesselberg. There are others too numerous to mention. They are attacking the Committee for doing its duty to protect this country and save the American people from the horrible fate the Communists have meted out to the unfortunate *Christian* people of Europe. [Emphasis added.]

For almost a year the Hollywood community and the Committee for the First Amendment gamely continued the fight—the bravest, most attractive, most generous, and by far the most vulnerable defenders of free speech the country had yet seen. Whatever position each of them held in the world had been achieved lonesomely, without institutional support or grants-in-aid, and their futures held no hope of tenure. They had sensed the House committee's purpose more accurately than the rest of the country, and were willing, at that time and in those circumstances, to stake their reputations in a fight against it.

What they did not expect, and could not have anticipated, was betrayal at the hands of the same intellectuals who had first instructed them in the liberal credo and the virtues of democratic action. They listened intently to the enormous silence that had fallen over the airwaves, the press, the theatre, the reviews, the universities, the academies. They knew, too late, exactly what it meant. Many of them in later years paid heavily for their misjudgment, and all of them were affected by it in one way or another, but while they lasted they made a light.

By 1949, when the Circuit Court of Appeals, to no one's surprise, ruled for the committee, the Ten had become objects of almost supersitious horror and execration. All channels of communication, aside from an occasional hired hall, were closed off to them, and even the hall was a sometime thing: when it wasn't cancelled altogether, it was packed to the eaves with stormily applauding agents of the FBI. Press relations, never good, turned lamentable, and even personal relations left something to be desired, as evidenced by the writer who jumped to his feet at a meeting of the Screen Writers' Guild, shouted "Beware of the bear! Beware of the bear!" and sat down as irrelevantly as he had stood up.

There were, of course, contrary voices. Bernard de Voto and Archibald MacLeish and Van Wyck Brooks and Professor Thomas I. Emerson of the Yale Law School tirelessly warned their confreres what the committee was doing, not primarily to the Ten, but to themselves and to the country, while men like

Harlow Shapley, Thomas Mann, Albert Einstein, and Linus Pauling, in addition to opposing the committee, associated themselves personally with those the committee hoped to imprison.

But personal support, however gratifying, was not the primary requirement. The liberal establishment simply could not be made to understand that the point at issue was not defense of the Ten but opposition to the committee; that it didn't matter whether the Ten were Communists, Nazis, homosexuals, or giraffes, what did matter was the committee's assertion of power in areas forbidden to it. They would learn the truth later, and ADA would muster fifty-eight votes against the committee in 1965, but that would be the result of changing generations and different battles. The first generation skipped the one that counted.

William F. Buckley, Jr., finding himself recently at odds with James Baldwin, knows exactly how to resolve these annoying differences of ideology and intellect: "How long," he wonders, "before the Baldwins will be ghettoized in the corners of fanaticism where they belong?" It's a lovely project, but Mr. Buckley himself is scarcely the one to bring it off. For that job you need a *sheep* in sheepskin, not a wolf.

It wasn't the committee or the American Legion or the DAR or Parnell Thomas or Francis Walter or Walter Judd or Joe McCarthy or Roy Cohn or Westbrook Pegler or George Sokolsky or Victor Riesel who convinced the liberal establishment that the best way to fight the committee was to "ghettoize" anyone who did; it was Arthur M. Schlesinger, Jr.'s "non-Communist Left" bursting out of the river and crossing the trees in its first wild stampede toward the Center, startling to their feet great herds of creeping Socialists while Max Eastman and Sidney Hook, riding the flanks and bearing down hard, fired buckshot and bacon-rind at the face of the wondering moon.

They were going so fast they overshot their mark, but toward dawn they found themselves in some pretty fair pastureland slightly to the Right of center. The grass was ankle-high, there was a stream to drink from and defecate into, the horses were winded and they were all bone-tired, so they decided to settle in permanently. Bugles blared, enlisted men stood at attention, censors swung great pots of diabolofuge, and the chief idealogue christened the place Vital Center. After the songs were finished they proclaimed a new alphabet and sent guerrilla bands fanning out through the countryside in all directions. They had been secretly trained to throw aspersions instead of cast them, their aim was deadly, and whenever they scored a hit they swarmed down on the poor devil and forced him to draw his own conclusions in the mire while everybody stood around and jeered. By the time they were through you couldn't cross the Charles River without three salutes and a police permit.

The only remaining support for the unwanted and unholy Ten lay in that sorely pressed coalition which emerged under Henry Wallace as the Progressive Party. It wasn't much, but it was enormously better than nothing. The committee and the press took the more sinister view that their sustenance came almost exclusively from the Communist Party, but as usual they hadn't the vaguest notion of what they were talking about. In New York City, which is the money capital of the country for everybody, including political mendicants, the national leaders of the Communist Party were backed up against almost every wall in town, bedeviled by more investigations, indictments, trials, and convictions than any dissident outfit really needs. In such circumstances, it didn't overmuch pleasure their hearts to discover some (still) well-suited member of the Ten prowling their precincts instead of his own in pursuit of Yankee dollars that stood in hideously shortening supply. Although they didn't picket the Ten, or gun them down, neither did they take joy in the sound of their approaching footsteps, nor steer them to those secret places where the big money broods on social injustice.

HUAC, too, had its problems. The massive purge it had planned and actually announced obviously couldn't be pulled off until the courts decided whether it had the right to pose the purgative, or $64, question which the Ten had challenged in the courts. A majority of law faculties and legal reviews predicted a reversal which would free the Ten and forbid the committee to pose the only interesting question it knew how to ask. Then in 1949, as the case passed upward for final disposition, Justices Murphy and Rutledge died in swift succession. The Supreme Court's liberal majority was diminished by two. Yet still the Committee did not move. It turned elsewhere, to be sure, but for thirty-two long months it made not so much as a feint toward the lush lands it had publicly staked out for its own. It was that near a thing. Then, as the summer of 1950 approached, the Supreme Court refused review; the power of the Congress to compel political revelation was legitimized; the Ten were swiftly distributed throughout the federal prison system—and the dam broke.

For a full decade thereafter the hunt raged at blood heat, roving wherever its masters wished, summoning whomever it pleased, demanding answers to questions never before heard in chambers that displayed the American flag—not, as some may have hoped, only in Hollywood (where over two hundred decent American citizens, including forty-four returned veterans, were humiliated, bankrupted, and driven from their professions), but in every area of American life that dealt with ideas and their dissemination.

What a curious era it was, and how sad: actors driven from radio, television, film, and theatre—their fellow actors working all the while; doctors removed from the registry of such hospitals as Cedars of Lebanon in Los Angeles—their colleagues never once considering a move *en masse* to more civilized quarters; professors, hounded from lecture halls, musicians from recording studios and symphony orchestras, artists from galleries and museums—their brothers contentedly continuing to teach, perform, exhibit; scientists banished from laboratories, ministers from pulpits, students from colleges, reporters from newspapers, editors from publishing houses, craftsmen from unions, lawyers, economists, sociologists, and statisticians from government posts; hundreds, perhaps even thousands of civil servants at every level insulted, destroyed, cast aside—and nothing, really, done about it, no cry in the streets that murder was afoot, nothing at all to be heard except a few cranks and do-gooders howling in vain to the rising wind. Colleagues, friends, fellow workers stepped softly into the jobs of the damned, and the hole which their disappearance left in the fabric of community life was scarcely noticed except when one of them killed himself or required commitment.

The eeriest aspect of a decade that lost its mind because men and women refused to take the national spotlight and swear they were or were not Communists, lay in the fact that a surprising number of those who declined the question had private yearnings to answer it and be damned to everyone.

The idea of compulsion, however, changed everything. For if Congress could compel public confession of political affiliation, it could also compel confession of candidates voted for, which would do queer things to the Australian, or—as we call it—secret ballot. Beyond this, there was the annoying moral quibble that compliance with the committee's request vastly simplified the task of detroying all who would not comply, or couldn't give the approved answer. In such a game the prize for winning seemed scarcely worth the trouble. Or perhaps one thought of all those good German intellectuals and artists and craftsmen who swore so eagerly they were not Jews and never had been. *Hals und Beinbruch!* as the toast goes.

In any event, error and contempt swept the field despite the feeling of many non-swearers that every aspect of a man's life is relevant to aesthetic evaluation of his work; that the more one knows about the life of a painter, the more one understands his painting; that, in fact, to study one and ignore the other is to diminish the available truth by half. Just so for writers: it makes a considerable—and by no means invidious—difference if one knows whether a book about hanging was written by the judge, the hangman, or the widow of a man who was hanged.

Granting that the amount of useful information varies from person to person, it would generally seem relevant to know the author's sex, race, nationality, age, religious belief or lack of it; and, in a time when politics invokes fiercer passions than religion and kills more people, what political group he belongs to. In an open society, a rational society, a society in which diversity is cherished rather than penalized, such information would be known to all as a matter of normal human intercourse.

Unhappily we do not have such a society in America, and with the exception of something that suggested its possibility during the Roosevelt years, we have not had for more decades than one cares to remember. France has it in degree at least, and England in larger degree. With local variations, Italy has it, and so do the Scandinavian countries. It is quite possible almost anywhere in Europe to find oneself at table with a priest, a Social-Democratic politico, a journalist of the Right or Center, a Communist novelist, a *rentier*, and an ex-resistance fighter turned salesman, each in lively disagreement with all except his hostess (whose deceased husband was suspected of collaboration) and none concealing the viewpoint from which he speaks or the goal to which he aspires.

Each election year in Italy the banner of the Communist Party hangs in its turn from the battlement of Castel Sant' Angelo, the Vatican's great citadel on the Tiber—yet only a thousand yards away the Pope still reigns, the saints and martyrs atop the Bernini Colonnade still marvelously praise both God and man.

They may not have our form of government, or a First Amendment, or a Supreme Court to interpret what it so plainly says, but most Europeans do have the right to join anything they wish and to shout their opinions and affiliations from the highest hill they can climb without fear of criminal prosecution or professional death. That is what an open society means, and what we do not have in America.

We do not have it because, taking from the Soviet

Union a tip that nearly destroyed it and drowned a whole generation in blood, we have transformed our politics into faith, our way of life into a religion, and our national purpose into a world crusade of absolute good against Satan's utter evil. Between such extremes there can be no dialogue, no agreement, and no peace until Satan is annihilated and communism vanishes from the face of the earth. In every area of his life we confront modern man with a choice of our absolute over Satan's. If he declines the choice, we isolate or bribe him until he acquiesces. If he chooses Satan's absolute, we kill him on the spot, or, if that be found inopportune, add his name to the lengthening list of those to be ministered unto at Armageddon. The first commandment of the new secular religion is to hate; its last commandment is to kill. We have heard them repeated so often in schools, churches, government, and press that no one dreams any longer of challenging the concept that brought them forth. By rote we have learned the faith and now by rote we believe it.

Beyond mere belief, we worship and fear it, and sustain it with processes more ritualistic than legal, tribal in nature, propitiatory, and sometimes magical. The committee, as inquisition, smokes out the heretic and hands him over to the secular arm of the courts for punishment. Ordeals of purification become mandatory for admission to the higher orders, confessions of faith to the lower. The community of the unbaptized suffers *arcani disciplina;* backsliders do penance through contrition, confession and satisfaction; diaboleptics are exorcised with great regularity, and permanently interdicted from fire and water if the treatment fails. A *Malleus maleficarum* issues annually from the Government Printing Office.

A new language of incantation grows up. Phrases like "international Communist conspiracy" and "slave world," repeated frequently enough and in precise word-order, have great value as spells to confound the enemy. "Free world," "free enterprise" and such function as charms for our side. We no longer confront the external world with ourselves as we are, but with our "image." Images as means of casting spells stand very high in the thaumaturgic lore. Today, however, images, effigies and statues are regarded as generically the same, differentiated no longer by what they do, but by what is done to them; i.e., a statue is looked at, an effigy is more often burned than not, and an image is venerated. The veneration, Webster says, is religious. Clearly, then, we present our image for the world's veneration. If it venerates, our spell has worked. If it doesn't, more powerful magic and better sorcerers will make a new image, one of such absolute bewitchment they'll have to venerate it whether they wish it or not. But stand before them as ourselves? Indeed not. They would steal our mana.

In this curious atmosphere of charms, oaths, and incantations, meanings have a way of becoming their opposites, values reverse themselves, tergiversation becomes the rule, and "pragmatic truth"—meaning a lie that works—stands much higher on the scale of virtue than simple truth that hurts. Is it, then, a matter of astonishment that the State Department denied we were making U-2 flights, or that we organized and supported the Bay of Pigs? Of course not. They were telling God's absolute pragmatic truth right up to the hour they were caught. And when mundane rather than theological truth finally stood revealed, it was not the lies we deplored, but the admissions of truths that exposed them.

With the fount of honor thus polluted at its source by a single word that changes everything and packs the killing power of a bullet, the simple act of staying out of trouble requires more guile than most men have on call. ". . . Mother Bloor is an old lady," said the witness to the committee's counsel. "Wouldn't you say an old *Communist* lady?" [*Emphasis added.*] "I certainly would," cried the witness, "I certainly would!" The word had to be inserted into the sentence with great delicacy, but once there it changed the old lady and the witness and the counsel, too.

Just so, they are not ordinary families we inadvertently incinerate in North and South Vietnam, they are *Communist* families (or families saved from communism), and that, somehow, excuses the inadvertence. Occasionally it has to be explained why we can't, or don't kill Communists. President Kennedy, that extraordinarily humane and graceful man, once felt obliged to explain to the press that it was the danger of killing Russian personnel, with consequent possibility of Soviet retaliation, that prevented us from bombing Cuban missile sites. The danger that we might kill a Cuban child wasn't discussed. It wasn't relevant.

Our faith accounts it a noble act for one to die for all. The idea that it may be nobler for all to die in defense of one—that this, indeed, is the whole meaning of brotherhood—finds no sanctuary in our hearts. If in fighting communism we find it necessary to kill a child, we will surely kill it. We have killed them already in substantial numbers. Exactly how many we do not know because we do not ask. We will continue to kill them as long as the word "Communist" triggers hatred and steels us to murder.

The whole degrading process of politics-as-magic and incantation-as-intellect will continue until that terrible word, "Communist," is wrested from sorcerers and robbed of its necromaneous power to drive us mad. It will not stop until all the orders and estates of the intellect—education, law, science, art, philosophy, religion—not just a few of them as in the past, but all of them together—rise to their feet and perform at last the function for which they were ordained, which is to speak the truth, the extremely simple truth without which reason and the rational world cannot survive: that there are no absolutes, neither absolute good nor absolute evil, neither absolute truth nor absolute falsehood; that all men partake of good and evil, and all faiths, and all nations; that—and this will be the hardest and bravest because it touches on the world that kills—there is a rational probability that Communists, as individual human beings, have as many (though possibly different) virtues as we ourselves; that just as our society is not completely good, neither is it likely that Communist society can be held completely evil; that in one area, at least—a determination to avoid being bombed from the face of the earth—both societies seek the same goal; and that common ends provide the surest basis for rational discussion of common means.

Even if such an improbable consensus of the estates occurred, the time may already be too late and the steadily diminishing area of allowable dissent too small for it to be effective. Five million voters in the Presidential campaign of 1924, declining a choice between Coolidge and Davis, distributed their votes among LaFollette and five other minority candidates. Forty years later the voters of thirty-six states, including the six most populous, had no third choice at all: it was Johnson-Goldwater or nothing. Three minority candidates got their names on the ballots of some of the remaining sixteen states, although none on all of them. Instead of 1924's five million votes, the minority candidates of 1964 polled fifty thousand. The dissenting independent vote had shrunk from 17 per cent of the electorate to .009 per cent in four decades. The radical Left had disappeared entirely: the radical Right had captured one of the two major political parties, and 26,000,000 Americans had voted for its candidate.

It was not only the radical Left that had disappeared: with it also had vanished the whole vigorous coalition of the general Left that had provided the sinews of four Presidential campaigns, and inspiration for a large body of New Deal legislation. In the area of organized political and legislative action, the ADA stands as far Left as the action goes, and it isn't Left at all, it's a coalition of the liberal Center. There remain only the peace marchers and the civil rights movement. The peace marchers want peace, and the civil rights organizations are out not to challenge the law but to enforce it; not to change the Constitution but to restore it. Neither is a political organization or a left-wing movement (July 1965), although civil violence and red-baiting could, at a decisive moment, turn each into both. For all practical purposes, however, the Left, as a movement proposing new ideas and decisive social change, doesn't live here any more.

The hard-headed, rock-ribbed gentlemen of the far American Right had known what they wanted all along, and their methods, though cruder and more brutal than their opponents', were expertly chosen for the job at hand. The anti-Communist campaign they had inaugurated on that cold January dawn in 1920 had been aimed at the entire leftwing of American political life, and only incidentally at Communists. Though the targets changed, the method didn't. The same weapon that blasted the incidental target wreaked such damage on the primary one that its defenders fell silent or vanished in retreat.

The whole campaign had been a fraud, and it still is. The American Communist Party, unarmed, fluid in its membership to the point of instability, outmanned 80,000 to 131,000,000 at its peak, posed about as grave a threat of revolution as the Ancient Arabic Order of the Nobles of the Mystic Shrine, which outmanned it ten to one and had much more fun. Until 1945 no one even suggested the possibility of a Soviet attack on the United States, and after that date, unless the military has lied to us for twenty years running, there hasn't been a day we couldn't overawe, over-bomb, over-kill and overwhelm not only Russia, but the rest of the world with her. It is not communism these amiable, soft-spoken, tribal epigones are out to destroy, it is the right of the majority of the American people to legislate in their own behalf. They mean to curb that right and control that majority, and they perfectly understand it will take the full power of the federal government to do the job. They propose to capture that power. They have created the weapon with which to do it, and the climate of insanity that suits it best. They will turn it against anyone who stands in their way. Far from fighting revolution, some of them already ponder one of their own. A legal one, of course. Perhaps something like . . .

Yet everywhere people tell me things are getting better. The sun comes up earlier these days, the blacklist tapers off, and children seem to be growing taller than they used to. Splendid sentiments flower in the most improbable gardens, and there's going to be the damnedest harvest in Appalachia you ever saw. They even let you read from your own books in the White House parlor, and with Hubert Humphrey where he is, there's an outside chance he may have an opportunity as President to fill with Communists the very concentration camps his sponsorship as Senator made possible. Everything comes up roses, the 1964 election was the greatest victory for our side that anyone has ever seen.

It was also the greatest victory *their* side has ever seen. Never before had the American far Right been able to carry its program to the whole people from the platform of a national party; never had a candidate of the Right been so attractive, or aroused such profound devotion; never before had hundreds of thousands of dollars—perhaps even millions—flowed to its cause from the "grass roots," that lost, embittered, isolated army of smallholders driven almost mad by the intolerable thought they were not rich, and never would be, and might, under the horrors of creeping socialism, Godless communism, do-goodism and the income tax, become even poorer.

Neither had it ever before received so many votes. There is an idiot theory abroad that 26,000,000 people voted for Mr. Goldwater in a sort of *crise de coeur,* hating his program but loving the GOP. The reverse seems closer to the truth. Those who couldn't stomach the program bolted: those who didn't bolt were not dragooned, they were either believers or opportunists. Between such there is no choice; their mutual attraction in a happy cause is so powerful that all distinctions vanish.

Each year a constellation of some 250 rich individuals, 100 business concerns, and 70 tax-exempt foundations pour between $25,000,000 and $35,000,000 into such organizations as the American Security Council, Americans for Constitutional Action, the Americanism Educational League, the American Conservative Union, the Congress of Conservatives, the Conservative Party of New York, the Freedom School (all you have to do is put in the word "freedom" and people send you $600,000 by return mail), the Freedom Foundation of Valley Forge, the Christian Freedom Foundation, Young Americans for Freedom, the Free Enterprise Bureau, the Free Society Association, the John Birch Society, the Constitution Party of Florida, the Liberty Lobby, the Cardinal Mindzenty Foundation, the Christian Anti-Communist Crusade, the Committee for the Monroe Doctrine, the National Defense Committtee of the D.A.R., the White Citizens' Councils in the South, the Americanism Committees of the various veteran groups, and innumerable regional societies of young, old, middle-aged, conservative, disillusioned, indignant, resurgent, frightened, or free Republicans.

Publications like the *National Review, American Opinion, Human Events, The Wanderer,* and the *Liberty Letter* promulgate doctrine for the scores of lesser journals and organizational publishing houses which flood the mails at every level, while *Washington Report, Life Line* (formerly *Facts Forum*), *Let Freedom Ring,* the Deering Milliken Foundation, the Penthouse Trust, and others spread or finance the word by radio, television, filmed shorts, and even telephone.

The vigor and variety and burgeoning health of the movement is somehow reminiscent of the great days of the Popular Front, with the exception that the Popular Front had no foothold in the police and military, and no secret bands of armed auxiliaries. The new Right, of course, has both. The political coloration of most peace officers' organizations, as well as those of the retired military, may be fairly judged by that of the 20,000-member National Sheriff's Association, which this year elected Sheriff James G. Clark of Selma, Alabama, its vice-president, assuring his automatic elevation to the presidency in 1966. Combine their forces in a time of crisis with such veterans' action groups as fought the labor wars of the twenties, and thousands of their like-minded brethren from the country's organized gun clubs, and riflemen's associations, and you have as formidable —and as legal—a political army as anyone could wish for.

Deeper in the shadows lurk the real Communist-hunters, the ones who carry guns. They have the special virtue that they can be disavowed or even denounced by their more respectable brethren and still hold firm, since they have no other place to go. They call themselves Councillors, Raiders, Minutemen, Vigilantes, Rangers, Volunteers, Kluxers, Nazis, and other names still more colorful. They are the mountain dwellers, the Scythians, men with hard eyes and emaciated spirits and terrible hungers, bigots, prophesiers, killers, night-prowlers, parading the flag as a hunting license, organizing combat-teams and counter-guerrilla details, spanning the country with counter-conspiratorial warfare schools, secret training camps, hidden ammunition depots, studying *A Handbook for Saboteurs* and *The Secret Principles of Guerrilla Warfare*—violent men fed on the violent words of their betters, and armed: armed with mortars, bazookas, bazooka rockets, rifle grenades, hand grenades, dynamite, guns, and hate.

They wait, all of them from high to low, and they prophesy crisis, which is to say they pray for it. They know the power of their weapon, and our fear of it, and even a small crisis is better than none. But what they especially dream of is a profound crisis, that anguished crisis of the spirit which tears us to pieces every thirty or forty years, one that will soften our hearts to the tall fierce strangers who stand outside the door and cry salvation. They are certain the door will open; they have no doubts at all that a time will come when the prevalence of devils will persuade us that freedom is best defended by surrendering it altogether.

And perhaps they are right. Perhaps we don't like freedom any more. Perhaps we have listened so long to the concatenation from the swamp that all unknowingly we have passed our point of no return, and now drift closer and closer to the heart of that thick, nadiral stupor in which men no longer want to be free. The cats have killed all the birds, the swimming pools everywhere overflow, and across the street at the old Bella Union—*che bella* that union was in her time, *che bellissima!*—the bar is closing down. The midnight air stutters with the magic word, and men with pinched white faces steal through the street. They have long memories, and the shortest tempers you ever saw, and they fondle guns instead of girls. Yet I do not dread them as much as I fear the others—the silent ones, the contented, the alienated, the frightened, the acquiescent.

I dream that for reasons I do not understand angry men are chasing me through the nightscape of a strange city. I duck into a side street and they do not. I come to a closed door and knock on it. There is no answer. The house is dark, yet I sense someone inside, someone standing "shadowless, like silence listening to silence." I hear sounds of the hunters retracing their steps. I cry my alarms to the silent listener inside. I beg refuge. He does not answer. The hunters whirl into my side street. I try to smash the door but it is too strong. The hunters race toward me. I cross to a window that is only partly draped. I cup hands to my brow and peer through it. The face in the darkness which stares so intently back at me is mine. The hunters strike. I waken.

Only then do I understand that I am of my own time. Only then do I fear that I am lost.